English

YEAR 3

Victoria Burrill

GALORE PARK

AN HACHETTE UK COMPANY

The Publishers would like to thank the following for permission to reproduce copyright material.

Photo credits

p4 © Belizar/Fotolia **p10** © Paul Tymon/Shutterstock **p18** © Steven Sullivan/Shutterstock **p25** © Yongyut Kumsri/Shutterstock **p31** © Adike/Shutterstock **p36** © Oleksandrserbinov/Shutterstock **p43** © Jules Frazier/Photodisc/Getty Images/Backgrounds Objects V08 **p46** © Comstock Images/Photolibrary Group Ltd/Concept Icons COM-3 KCD-00055 **p53** © NASA/Yuri Arcurs/Fotolia **p57** © Mike Brown/Fotolia **p64** © Valentino Nobile/Shutterstock **p75** ©PA Photos/TopFoto **p80** © Zurijeta/Shutterstock **p89** © Walt Disney/Amblin Entertainment/Photo 12/Alamy Stock Photo **p93** © Grand Warszawa/Shutterstock **p98** © Best dog photo/Shutterstock **p105** © Tatiana Murr/Shutterstock **p113** © Peter Byrne/PA Wire/PA Images

Acknowledgements

p4 from *Animal Friends* by Dick King-Smith, published by Walker Books (permission sought) **p5** First published 1998 by Kingfisher, an imprint of Pan Macmillan, a division of Macmillan Publishers International Limited. Text copyright © Macmillan Publishers International Limited 2004. (used with permission) **p16** Jamila Gavin, "Three Indian Princesses". Published by Egmont Books Limited. Used with permission. **p17** From *The Changing Face of India* by David Cumming. First published in UK by Wayland, an imprint of Hachette Children's Books, Carmelite House, 50 Victoria Embankment, London EC4Y ODZ (used with permission) **p28** Roald Dahl, "The Witches". Published by Penguin Books. Used with permission. **p31** From How to train your dragon by Cressida Cowell, first published in the UK by Hodder Children's Books, an imprint of Hachette Children's Books, Carmelite House, 50 Victoria Embankment, London imprint, EC4Y 0DZ. Used with permission from Hodder Children's Books and David Higham Associates Ltd. Text and illustrations copyright © 2003 by Cressida Cowell. Used by permission of Little Brown Books for Young Readers. **p41** Reproduced from *Treasure Island* by permission of Usborne Publishing, 83-85 Saffron Hill, London EC1N 8RT, UK. www.usborne.com. Copyright © 2007 Usborne Publishing Ltd **p43** First published 1998 by Kingfisher, an imprint of Pan Macmillan, a division of Macmillan Publishers International Limited. Text copyright © Macmillan Publishers International Limited 2004. (used with permission) **p51** by Alan Hammond (used with permission of the author) **p52** From HISTORY NEWS: IN SPACE by Michael Johnstone. Text © 1999 Michael Johnstone. Reproduced by permission of Walker Books Ltd, London SE11 5HJ. www.walker.co.uk **p62** The Literary Executor of Leonard Clark for "Good Company" by Leonard Clark. © Leonard Clark. (used with permission) **p63** from *e.explore: Insect* by David Burnie, published by Dorling Kindersley and Google (permission sought) **p74** My Story: The Blitz. Text Copyright @ Vince Cross, 2001. Reproduced by permission of Scholastic Ltd. All rights reserved. **p77** My Story: Pompeii. Text Copyright © Sue Reid 2008. Reproduced by permission of Scholastic Ltd. All rights reserved. **p86** Roald Dahl, "The BFG". Published by Penguin Books. Used with permission. **pps88, 92 and 93** Roald Dahl and David Wood, "The BFG: Plays for Children". Published by Penguin Books. Used with permission. **p98** Extracts from www.rspca.org.uk. Used with permission. **p99** from www.express.co.uk (used with permission) **p110** From The Butterfly Lion. Reprinted by permission of HarperCollins Publishers Ltd © 1996 Michael Morpurgo. **p113** © Telegraph Media Group Limited 2016 (used with permission) **p118** OXFORD SCHOOL THESAURUS (2007) edited by Robert Allen. By permission of Oxford University Press, UK.

Every effort has been made to trace all copyright holders, but if any have been inadvertently overlooked, the Publishers will be pleased to make the necessary arrangements at the first opportunity.

Although every effort has been made to ensure that website addresses are correct at time of going to press, Galore Park cannot be held responsible for the content of any website mentioned in this book. It is sometimes possible to find a relocated web page by typing in the address of the home page for a website in the URL window of your browser.

Hachette UK's policy is to use papers that are natural, renewable and recyclable products and made from wood grown in sustainable forests. The logging and manufacturing processes are expected to conform to the environmental regulations of the country of origin.

Orders: **Teachers** please contact Bookpoint Ltd, 130 Park Drive, Milton Park, Abingdon, Oxon OX14 4SE. Telephone: (44) 01235 400555. Email primary@bookpoint.co.uk. Lines are open from 9 a.m. to 5 p.m., Monday to Saturday, with a 24-hour message answering service.

Parents, Tutors please call: 020 3122 6405 (Monday to Friday, 9:30am–4.30pm). Email: parentenquiries@galorepark.co.uk

Visit our website at www.galorepark.co.uk for details of other revision guides for Common Entrance, examination papers and Galore Park publications.

ISBN: 978 1 4718 8215 9

© Victoria Burrill 2017

First published in 2017 by
Galore Park Publishing Ltd,
An Hachette UK Company
Carmelite House
50 Victoria Embankment
London EC4Y 0DZ
www.galorepark.co.uk

Impression number   10 9 8 7 6 5 4

Year   2021 2020

Cover photo © nambitomo/Getty Images/iStockphoto

Illustrations by Aptara, Inc.

Typeset in India

Printed in Dubai

A catalogue record for this title is available from the British Library.

Contents

Introduction

Reading unlocks the world. Reading newspaper and magazine articles provides you with valuable information about what is going on around you, reading letters and diary extracts allows you to share the thoughts and experiences of other people, and reading stories and poems unlocks your imagination and lets you fly freely to places, spaces and times you may never be able to visit in real life. And being able to retrieve and summarise what you have read, to understand the structure and purpose of a text and why an author has used the language they have used, and to infer meaning and make deductions from what you have read are the keys to reading. In turn, reading helps you learn how to speak, how to listen and how to write; how to communicate your own thoughts, feelings and ideas with those around you.

This series adopts a skills-based approach to teaching English. This means that you will be introduced to a skill, such as the comprehension skill of inference or how to write a descriptive passage, and you will return to it throughout Years 3 to 6, getting better and better at it over time.

⮕ Notes on features

You will come across the following features that are designed to help you:

Skill focus

This box will explain the comprehension skill each chapter focuses on.

This box points you to the reading list for each chapter. The reading lists can be found in *English Year 3 Answers* (available as a PDF download from the Galore Park website – ISBN 9781471896644).

In these boxes you will come across questions to help you:

- practise your comprehension skills
- practise using grammar correctly
- practise using punctuation correctly
- practise your spelling
- develop your vocabulary
- practise your creative writing skills.

Speaking and listening

These activities will help you develop your speaking and listening skills.

The hedgerow

Hedgerows are fascinating places, full of busy little creatures and creepy crawlies. Some fantastic stories have been written about hedgerows and a hedgerow is also a great setting for a story of your own. Imagine all the adventures the hedgerow creatures could get up to!

Skill focus: Retrieval

In this chapter you will learn how to spot a question that asks you to find information in a text. You will then practise finding the correct information.

A reading list of books about animals can be found in *English Year 3 Answers*.

➲ Comprehension

For all comprehension exercises you should begin by reading through the passage. You do this to make sure you know what it is about and that you can understand it.

Next, you should look at the questions, read them through and start to think about what the answers might be. From reading the passage, you might remember some of the answers, or remember where to find them.

Finally, you should go back to the text and try to find the answers to the questions.

Some of the questions you will come across will be retrieval questions. Some dogs, like Labradors, are called retrievers, because they are sent to find things and bring them back. In the same way, retrieval questions ask you to find a specific piece of information in the text and write it in the answer.

Retrieval questions often include the following phrases:

- Who was ...?
- Where is ...?
- When did ...?
- What was ...?
- Find and copy ...
- List ...

To answer retrieval questions, follow these steps:

1 Look at the question and work out what the answer will contain. For example, if it asks 'Who?', then the answer will be a name. If it asks 'Where?', then the answer will be a place.

2 Try to remember where in the text you think the answer is.

OR

Scan the text to find the section that contains the answer. You can do this by looking for important words. For example, if the question is about Mr Jones, look for his name. If it is about what time something happened, look for 'o'clock' or numbers.

3 Once you have found the correct part of the text, scan your eyes along the lines quickly to try to spot the right words.

4 Use the words in the question, to help you write your answer. For example, your answer to the question, 'What is the boy's name?', should begin, 'The boy's name is ...'.

Scanning is an important skill, which you will always use in comprehension exercises. It means reading something quickly to find specific pieces of information.

1 To practise scanning, time yourself for one minute and count how many times the letters 'sh' are written in the passage below:

> Sarah was sure that she had remembered to shut the front door. She thought back to the morning. After her shower, she had put on her shorts and short-sleeved shirt and gone downstairs. She had found a stray cat in the back garden, shouted at it and ushered it over the fence. Then she came back indoors, switched off the lights and shoved the dirty dishes into the dishwasher. She put the milk back on the shelf in the fridge and shut the fridge door, then went into the hallway and put on her shoes. Her keys were nowhere to be found and she shook every coat on the hook, hoping to hear them jangle. They were not there and she shrugged, unsure of where to search next. Suddenly she saw a shiny shape in the shadows on the floor. Her keys! She must have dropped them yesterday. Smiling, she opened the front door, pulled it behind her and stuck the key in the lock. Yes, she had definitely shut the front door!

Now look at these questions. The important words, which you should scan for, are underlined.

2 Which <u>clothes</u> does Sarah put on after her <u>shower</u>?

Here you might scan for 'shower' because you know she put her clothes on after her shower. You might also scan for different types of clothes.

3 How does Sarah get rid of the <u>cat</u>?

Scan for the word 'cat' and reread the part of the text where Sarah saw the cat. Make sure you read all of that part and find out everything she did.

4 Where does Sarah find her <u>keys</u> in the end?

Here you should scan for the word 'keys'. You might find it more than once so make sure you scan carefully so you can spot when she actually finds them.

5 How do you know Sarah is <u>pleased</u> to find her keys?

Here you need to scan for words that suggest she was pleased. Think about other words for 'pleased', such as 'happy', 'smile' and 'glad'.

> Now try to answer these questions yourself.

Try this comprehension exercise. Retrieval questions, where you need to use the scanning technique you have practised, are in bold.

Badger biffing

Never upset a badger. As Dick King-Smith knows, they can be full of surprises …

I bet there aren't many people who can say, 'Once I biffed a badger on the bottom with my hat.'

5 I can. I was going out early one summer's morning to fetch the cows in for milking. On my way I had to cross a big pasture, and there, right in the middle of it, was a badger.

10 Now, badgers are nocturnal animals and, though there was a big sett in the nearby wood where we often heard them clucking and chattering at night, it wasn't often that we saw them in broad daylight.

So I hurried towards this solitary badger, hoping that it wouldn't run away till I'd had a
15 good look at it. It didn't run away. It didn't take the slightest notice of me, even though I was now standing right beside it. It just carried on snuffling about in the grass.

I felt rather foolish. I took off my hat and biffed the badger gently on its bottom.

It didn't even look up. 'What's up with you, my friend?' I said. 'You deaf, or blind, or both?'

20 Slowly, with that rolling bear-like shuffle that badgers have, it began to move towards the wood, while I continued to beat a light tattoo on its backside. Until, at last, it came to a hole in the hedge, and disappeared.

The very next morning I went exactly the same way to fetch the dairy herd, and there, in exactly the same place, were two badgers. My friend, I thought, and his friend!

25 Happily I ran towards them. With a volley of furious grunts, the two badgers charged at me. I fled at top speed.

Nobody ever believes this story.

But it's true.

From *Animal Friends* by Dick King-Smith

6 **What is the author on his way to do when he sees the badger?**

7 **Where is the badger?**

8 **How does the badger react to the author, the first time he sees him?**

9 **Do you think the badger is frightened of the author the first time he sees him? Why or why not?**

10 **Why does the author think the badger might be 'deaf, or blind, or both'?**

11 **When does the author return to the place where he first saw the badger?**

Speaking and listening

12 Play 20 questions. Think of an animal and invite your friends to guess what it is. They may ask up to 20 questions and you must answer each question with only 'yes' or 'no'.

Now try this exercise. It is a non-fiction comprehension exercise, which is a common place to find retrieval questions that require you to scan the text for information.

Garden friends

How well do you know the animals in your garden? Here are some fascinating facts about a few of them.

Badger Badgers are powerful creatures, but they are also shy. They are related to skunks and, like them, have black and white markings. In Europe, they live in family groups in woodlands. Badgers are most active in the evening. This is when they come out to feed and to collect straw for bedding.

5 **Bat** Bats have big ears, furry bodies and wings like leather. They are nocturnal mammals. This means they sleep in caves and attics during the day and fly out to feed at night-time.

Hedgehog	Hedgehogs are mammals found in the woods and hedges of Europe, Asia and Africa. Most have thousands of thick spines covering their backs, which help to protect them from predators. There are also hairy hedgehogs, which live in Asia.
Mole	Moles are small mammals that spend almost all their lives underground. We know they are around because of the molehills they create when digging their tunnels. They live in Europe, Asia and North America. Big powerful front paws, a pointed nose and sharp claws mean that moles are excellent diggers.
Owl	Owls are birds of prey that hunt mainly at night. They use their sensitive hearing and large eyes (which give them good night vision) to catch animals such as mice and rabbits. Owls have soft feathers that allow them to fly silently. The hooting cry of some species is easy to recognise.
Squirrel	Most squirrels have big, bushy tails and live in trees. They are active during the day, running from branch to branch in search of nuts, fruit and seeds. Squirrels love seeds like acorns, which they gnaw with their sharp front teeth. In autumn, they sometimes bury a supply in the ground to last them through the winter.

From *First Encyclopedia of Animals by John Farndon and Jon Kirkwood*

13 What is similar about badgers and skunks?

14 Where are you most likely to find a bat during the daytime?

15 How do hedgehogs protect themselves from predators?

16 How would you know if there were moles in your garden?

17 Why are owls very good at catching mice and rabbits, even at night?

18 How are squirrels able to feed during the cold winter months?

19 If you could be any of the animals in the text, which would it be and why?

Speaking and listening

20 Find out about a garden animal, such as a fox, a squirrel or a mouse, and give a class talk on it. Find out about what it eats, where it sleeps, how long it lives for and other interesting facts. Present your talk to the class using pictures, as well as words, to keep everyone interested.

➡ Grammar

In this section you will look at different types of nouns, including collective nouns and proper nouns.

Nouns

A noun is the name of a person, a place or a thing. For example:

hedge   door   garden

These are called common nouns because they are the general name for things. Language is full of common nouns. Look at this sentence, from the first passage you read. The common nouns have been underlined:

I took off my <u>hat</u> and biffed the <u>badger</u> gently on its <u>bottom</u>.

In this sentence from the second passage you read, the underlined words are the names of places. These are called proper nouns and need to begin with a capital letter:

Hedgehogs are mammals found in the woods and hedges of <u>Europe</u>, <u>Asia</u> and <u>Africa</u>.

Proper nouns are the words for specific, one-of-a-kind places, people or things. For example:

- People: James, Queen Elizabeth, Mr Taylor
- Places: Spain, Paris, Lincolnshire, Jupiter
- Things: Coca Cola, January, River Severn, Mount Everest

Be careful: seasons are not classified as proper nouns.

Sometimes we need a noun for a group of similar things. These are called collective nouns. For example:

A group of lions is called a <u>pride</u>.

A group of wolves is called a <u>pack</u>.

21 Copy these sentences and underline the common nouns:

(a) The author met a badger in a field.

(b) The badger returned the next day with a friend.

(c) Bats have big ears, furry bodies and wings like leather.

(d) Bats sleep in caves and attics during the day.

(e) Hedgehogs have thick spines covering their backs.

(f) Most squirrels have big, bushy tails and live in trees.

22 Copy out these sentences, adding capital letters to the start of the proper nouns:

(a) Squirrels are found in africa, asia and europe.

(b) The author dick king-smith writes many books about garden creatures.

(c) One of his most popular stories is called the hodgeheg.

(d) Hedgehogs hibernate from november to march.

(e) The wildlife trust is a charity in the united kingdom, which works to conserve hedgerow animals.

23 Match up the animal with its collective noun. Use a dictionary to help you.

(a) ants		(i)	pod
(b) bees		(ii)	shoal
(c) geese		(iii)	clutch
(d) dolphins		(iv)	swarm
(e) fish		(v)	warren
(f) rabbits		(vi)	colony
(g) chicks		(vii)	herd
(h) cows		(viii)	flock

➔ Punctuation

In this section, you will practise basic sentence punctuation.

Capital letters and full stops

In English, every sentence must start with a capital letter. A full stop shows that the sentence has finished.

Look at these examples from the passages you read:

Moles are small mammals that spend almost all their lives underground.

Nobody ever believes this story.

24 Copy out these sentences, adding in the missing capital letters and full stops:

(a) hedgerows provide a place to live for many different creatures

(b) many birds build their nests in hedges

(c) they mark the boundary between fields

(d) hedges protect the soil in fields from the wind

25 Capital letters have been put in the wrong places in these sentences. Copy out these sentences, correcting them:

(a) the Ditches next to hedgerows provide a home for Toads and Frogs.

(b) berries grow on Hedges and provide food for Birds.

(c) farmers trim hedges to keep them in Good Condition.

(d) some Hedges are protected by Law.

26 Copy out the passage below, adding in the missing full stops and capital letters. You should end up with five sentences.

The fox is a member of the dog family there are many species of fox and a female fox is called a vixen they are found all over the world in both cities and in the countryside their home is called a den and they eat just about anything including worms, berries, spiders and even small mammals like mice if they have extra food, they hide it underground for later

➔ Spelling

When there is more than one of a noun, we use a plural version of the noun. For example:

one rabbit   becomes   two rabbits

one fox   becomes   three foxes

one sheep   becomes   four sheep

There are several important spelling rules to remember when making a noun plural. For most nouns, you just add an -s:

one beetle ⟶ two beetles   one ant ⟶ two ants

However:

- If the noun ends in -y with a consonant before it, remove the -y and add -ies. For example:

    fly ⟶ flies   puppy ⟶ puppies

- If the noun ends in a -y with a vowel before it, just add -s. For example:

    monkey ⟶ monkeys   donkey ⟶ donkeys

- If a noun ends in -f, remove the -f and add -ves. For example:

    wolf ⟶ wolves   calf ⟶ calves

    Although there are a few exceptions: roofs, chiefs.

- If a noun ends in -o, then add -es. For example:

    hero ⟶ heroes   tomato ⟶ tomatoes

    The exceptions here are mostly words from other languages, such as pianos and mosquitos.

- If a word ends in a soft sound like -ch, -s, -sh or -x, then add -es. For example:

    fox ⟶ foxes   finch ⟶ finches

- Some words don't change at all and you need to remember these. For example:

    sheep   deer   fish

- Some words change completely and you need to remember these too. For example:

    mouse ⟶ mice   goose ⟶ geese
    child ⟶ children

■ A family of field mice

27 Write the plural for the following words:

(a) snake (d) hedge (g) brush

(b) match (e) potato (h) story

(c) box (f) leaf (i) tooth

28 Write the singular word that these plurals come from:

(a) countries (d) fields (g) women

(b) bunches (e) grasses (h) bunnies

(c) valleys (f) trees (i) buses

→ Vocabulary

Creatures in the hedgerow come in all shapes and sizes. Think about how we might describe things that are big and small.

29 Sort the following words into two groups: one for words meaning big and one for words meaning small. Use a dictionary to help you.

miniature mammoth miniscule giant tiny
great substantial mini immense diminutive
teeny baby enormous sizable colossal

30 Use some of the words above to write sentences about different animals. For example: The miniscule field mouse hid in the hedgerow.

Speaking and listening

31 With a partner, imagine you are two squirrels getting ready for winter. What might you do? What might you talk about? Create a short role play to show to the class.

→ Writing

In this section you are going to practise writing short stories. Use the following simple steps to help you:

1 Choose two animal characters. Sometimes it's more interesting if the characters are quite different from one another.

2 Choose a setting. Where might you find these types of characters?

3 Think of a problem or challenge that they might face. It should match up with the kind of characters and the setting you have chosen.

4 Decide how you want your story to end. Will it have a happy ending? How will the characters solve the problem or complete the challenge?

Here is an example of how to plan and start a short story:

Don't forget to use speech to show what the characters talk about.

Introduce the first character.

Characters: A hedgehog and a mouse

Setting: A woodland in the country

Problem: The mouse is hurt and can't get back to his burrow. The hedgehog can't carry him because his spines will hurt the mouse even more.

Ending: The hedgehog rolls in leaves to cover his spines and safely carries the mouse home.

As Mr Hedgehog was strolling home with a full tummy after successfully foraging for food, he thought he heard a strange squeaking sound. He looked around him. It was autumn, and the red, orange and brown leaves lay on the floor like a colourful carpet. The sun was beginning to set and it was getting darker. He couldn't see any other creatures so he continued walking home. Then he heard a feeble voice behind him, 'H-h-h-help me. Please.' He quickly turned, peered into the crunchy leaves, and saw a tiny white face almost buried among them. It seemed to be a tiny field mouse with tears in his eyes.

Introduce the second character.

Describe the setting.

Now try to plan and write these stories using the same simple steps to help you.

32 Write a story about two woodland or garden creatures.

33 Write a story in which two characters start off disliking each other and end up being friends. They could be people or animals.

34 Write a story with two characters: one is a child and the other is an animal.

35 Write a story in which the two characters are related. They might be brothers or sisters, or a parent and child. You can decide whether your characters are animals or people.

Indian adventure

India is a colourful and exotic place, full of amazing sights and sounds. Although it is a long way away, reading stories set in India and non-fiction books about India can help you travel there in your imagination, and help you think about what life is like on the other side of the world.

Skill focus: Inference

In this chapter you will learn how to write answers to inference questions by finding clues in the text. Inferring means working something out from a clue. For example, when your teacher stomps into the room with a frown and a grunt, you infer that he or she is in a bad mood. Perhaps someone forgot their homework!

A reading list of books about far-flung corners of the world can be found in *English Year 3 Answers*.

→ Comprehension

The answers to inference questions aren't obvious. You have to work them out, finding one or more pieces of information, thinking about what you have found, and then coming up with an answer.

Here is an example passage and some simple steps to help you understand how to answer inference questions:

It was Timmy's first day at school and he was very nervous. He had many friends at his old school, the headmistress was kind and funny and he was sad to leave when his family had to move to another city because of his dad's job. His old school was small but this new school seemed enormous. How would he ever get to know anybody? As he walked through the gates he heard a stern voice. 'Tuck in your shirt! You look a mess already and it's only 9 a.m.' The teacher in front of him glared at him as he fumbled with his shirt. Not a great start. As she stalked off, he heard another voice.

'Hi there. Are you new? What class are you in?' A smiling boy appeared in front of him.

'I'm in 4D, I think.'

'Me too. Follow me. My name's Sanjay,' and the smiling boy put his hand on Timmy's shoulder and led him into a classroom at the end of the corridor. As he walked inside, Timmy shuddered. At the front, with a grumpy look on her face and a nasty frown was the teacher who had told him off earlier. 'Sit down. You're late,' the teacher barked. Timmy shuffled to the nearest seat. 'Not there! At the back. Hurry up!'

1 Do you think Timmy's new teacher is friendly?

1 Look at the question and work out what it is asking about.

This question is about the boy's teacher and her personality.

2 Look in the text for the key words.

Look for the word 'teacher' and look for any words that might suggest whether she is friendly or not.

3 Think about the clues you have found and decide whether the teacher seems friendly or not.

4 When you write you answer, give a reason why you think she is friendly or not. Use one of the clues for this.

I don't think that Timmy's new teacher is friendly because she had a grumpy look on her face.

Now try to answer these questions using the steps above to help you.

2 Do you think Timmy liked his old school?

3 What kind of person do you think Sanjay is?

Try this comprehension exercise. Inference questions are in bold.

An Indian princess

This is a story about an adventurous Indian princess who wants to explore the world beyond the palace walls.

Savitri was a beautiful princess who lived in India hundreds of years ago. Her eyes were like lotus flowers. Her skin was the colour of sunbeams. Her hair was shining and long and as black as night. Her sarees[1] were made of the very finest silks, and she was always covered in jewels.

5   Her home was a magnificent palace with large beautiful rooms to explore, and cool courtyards with fountains in which to rest. And all around were the palace gardens with their intricate flower beds, avenues of cypress trees, and shady paths among the guava groves. But over the walls where the sun always set, where the rest of the world spread away to the shimmering horizon; over the wall was the jungle.

10   Savitri could see the jungle from her balcony. She could hear the jungle from her bed. Each morning she loved to watch the green parrots burst upwards from the tree tops into the pink, dawn sky and swoop round the palace. She loved to catch a glimpse of the spotted deer as they sprang through the dappled shadows; or the grey mongoose spinning and curling down the old, gnarled trunks of the trees.

15   Sometimes she saw a small solemn boy herding dusty buffalo down to the river. Sometimes she saw the village children running almost naked through the long grass only to disappear laughing and squealing into the jungle. How she longed to throw off her fine clothes and join them. How she longed to fling off her leather sandals and feel more than the hard, white marble beneath her feet.

20   One afternoon when her old ayah[2] was dozing in the heat of day, the gardener was bent intently over his rose bushes, and her chosen playmates were quarrelling on the swing, Savitri slipped away. From her balcony, she had often noticed a small door in the palace walls. Savitri was determined now to find this door. Hoisting up her saree, she ran through the palace gardens until she reached the high, grey boundary walls. Then
25   trailing her fingers along its ancient stones, she walked and walked for several minutes.

Suddenly, there it was. Just a small, wooden door. The only thing that stood between her and the outside world. She pushed and it opened. For a few moments Savitri stood absolutely still, just gazing in wonder. There was the jungle not more than three paces away, green and dense and very, very wild.

Adapted from *Three Indian Princesses* by Jamila Gavin

[1] saree or sari = a long garment worn by Indian women

[2] ayah = a nursemaid in India

4 Is the princess rich? How do you know?

5 Find two other phrases that show that 'Savitri was a beautiful princess'.

6 Do you think the princess is happy living in the palace? How do you know?

7 Which of these words do you think best describes Savitri? Give a reason for your choice.

lazy   curious   shy

8 Name three animals that Savitri can see from her balcony.

9 What do you think the princess is interested in? Why do you think this?

10 What do you think will happen next? Give a reason why you think this.

Speaking and listening

11 Take turns to be Savitri, or another person in the 'Indian princess' passage, and sit in the 'hot seat' at the front of the class. Answer questions from your classmates, in the role of that person. Try to imagine how he or she might answer each question.

Now try this comprehension exercise. The passage is an information text.

Living in India

India is a colourful, exciting and historic country, full of different people and places. Find out what modern India means to Rati, Suraj and Bhupinder.

I'm Rati Fyzee and I was born in Bombay in 1922. It has recently had its name changed to Mumbai, but I will always call it Bombay. That's its proper name!

My city has changed beyond all recognition since the 1970s. So many high-rise buildings have sprung up, Bombay has become the Manhattan of India. The city is
5   on a small peninsula, so we have had to build upwards rather than outwards on to neighbouring land.

All this building work has caused a lot of problems, particularly a leap in the
10   population. The people who came here to build the new offices and flats have stayed here, and now our slums are among the
15   largest in the world.

■ Mumbai, India

***

My name is Suraj. I'm 12 years old and I live in the capital city, New Delhi. We live in a block
20   of flats with a hundred other families. During the summer it gets very hot and there are always power cuts, because everyone has their air-conditioners and fans working flat out. We have a huge diesel generator that provides electricity when there is a power cut but the trouble is, it often breaks down. Then I miss my favourite TV serials. My mother says
25   it's a good opportunity to do my homework – by candlelight!

At school we have been learning about alternative power such as solar energy. We have so much sunshine in India that I think in future the government should use it to provide more electricity.

***

My name is Bhupinder and I live with my parents, my grandmother and four
30   brothers and sisters. In India there are too many people and not enough homes. We are too poor to buy a house or flat, so we have to rent a room from my father's boss. It's 3 metres wide and 4 metres long – a tight fit for eight people, but we manage.

My mother cooks outside in the yard. There's also a hand-pump here for our water. Life is very hard for us. Every day I see how lucky other families are and hope and
35   pray that I can get a good job so that I can look after my parents when they are old.

From *The Changing Face of India* by David Cumming

12 Which of the three speakers is the oldest?

13 According to Rati, how has his city changed? Find two ways it has changed.

14 Explain in your own words why the building work in Bombay has caused problems.

15 Which of the following words do you think best describes Suraj? Give a reason for your answer.

positive   lonely   angry

16 Explain in your own words why Suraj and his family experience lots of power cuts in the summer.

17 Which of the three speakers do you think has the hardest life? Give a reason for your answer.

18 Would you like to live in India? Give a reason for your answer.

Speaking and listening

19 Put together a short presentation – either on your own or with a partner – about a country that you would like to travel to one day. What do you like about this country? Do some research in the library or on the internet and share some information about the country, and explain why you would like to visit it.

→ Grammar

In this section you will find out how to use adjectives and adverbs to make your writing more interesting.

Adjectives

Adjectives are describing words. They tell the reader more about a noun, more about what it looks like and what kind of thing it is. For example:

the spotted deer

a small, wooden door

If you use more than one adjective, put a comma between them.

Often, you write the adjective before the noun but not always. For example:

Her hair was shining and long.

The adjectives still describe her hair, even though they come after the noun 'hair'.

20 Copy out these sentences and underline the adjectives.

(a) Savitri was a rich princess.

(b) Each morning she loved to watch the green parrots.

(c) Sometimes she saw a small, solemn boy herding dusty buffalo down to the river.

(d) How she longed to fling off her leather sandals and feel more than the hard, white marble beneath her feet.

(e) There was the jungle, green and dense and wild.

21 Copy out these sentences, adding some adjectives to make them more interesting.

(a) The princess walked through the garden.

(b) The children jumped into the river.

(c) The gardener picked the flowers.

(d) She lived in a palace with many rooms, a garden, fountains and a view of the jungle.

(e) The jungle was full of animals.

Adverbs

Adverbs are also describing words. They tell you more about a verb (doing word) and show the reader how or when something was done. For example:

The princess ran quickly through the garden.

The adverb **quickly** tells you how fast the princess ran.

The princess gazed thoughtfully at the door.

The adverb **thoughtfully** tells you how the girl looked at the door.

Many (but not all) adverbs end in -ly.

22 Copy out these sentences and underline the adverbs.

   (a) Savitri stepped cautiously into the garden.

   (b) The gardener tended carefully to the rose bushes.

   (c) Savitri tried hard to find a way into the jungle.

   (d) Deer and mongoose moved energetically through the trees.

   (e) The birds sang musically in the trees.

23 Copy out these sentences, adding some adverbs to make them more interesting.

   (a) The buffalo drank from the river.

   (b) Savitri's ayah slept in the shade.

   (c) The children played in the long grass.

   (d) She pushed the door.

   (e) The sun shone on the garden.

➔ Punctuation

In this section you will learn how to use apostrophes when two words are combined to make one word. This is called a contraction.

Apostrophes for contraction

An apostrophe looks like this: ' . One of the things it is used for is to show when two words have been squeezed together (contracted) by missing out some letters. You put the apostrophe where the letters are missing. For example:

   I'm Rati Fyzee and I was born in Bombay.

   There's a hand-pump for our water.

   My mother says it's a good opportunity to do my homework.

I'm is short for **I am**. The words have been squeezed together and the 'a' has been missed out. **There's** is short for **there is** and **it's** is short for **it is**.

Here are some of the most common contractions. The letters that have been squeezed out are in bold.

we **are** → we're   he **ha**d → he'd   I **have** → I've

do **not** → don't   they **will** → they'll   can **not** → can't

could **not** → couldn't   did **not** → didn't

---

24 Write down the contractions for the following words:

    (a) you will   **(d)** you have

    (b) will not   **(e)** where is

    (c) would not

25 Write out these sentences without contractions.

    (a) They'll be late.   **(d)** I'd like to see the jungle.

    (b) What's the time?   **(e)** It'll be sunny tomorrow.

    (c) She's a princess.

→ Spelling

A suffix is a set of letters that you add to the end of a word to change its meaning. The -ly suffix turns an adjective (a word that describes a noun) into an adverb (a word that describes a verb).

For most adjectives you just add -ly onto the end. For example:

    quick + ly = quickly

    careful + ly = carefully

    brave + ly = bravely

If the adjective ends in a -y, you change the -y to an -i, then add -ly. For example:

    sleepy + ly = sleepily

    angry + ly = angrily

    happy + ly = happily

26 Change these adjectives into adverbs by adding -ly. Don't forget the rules you learnt above.

(a) rude   (c) usual   (e) successful

(b) soft   (d) grumpy

27 Change these adjectives into adverbs and then use each one in a sentence.

(a) normal   (c) easy   (e) sad

(b) painful   (d) greedy

→ Vocabulary

In the passage you read about Princess Savitri, there were many animals in the jungle. Different animals move in different ways and it is important to know lots of verbs (doing words) to describe exactly how they move.

28 Find the following verbs in the dictionary and write a definition of each one.

(a) waddle   (e) pounce   (i) scamper

(b) slither   (f) lumber   (j) glide

(c) flutter   (g) stomp

(d) swoop   (h) prowl

29 For each verb in question 28, think of an animal that moves in that way and write a sentence including the animal and the verb.

Speaking and listening

30 Imagine that you are Princess Savitri. You have just returned to the palace after sneaking into the jungle for a while. Your nursemaid (ayah) is waiting for you, and she looks very angry! Working with a partner, role-play a conversation between Savitri and her ayah.

⬦ Writing

In this section you will be writing descriptions of different places, using the adjectives and adverbs you have been practising to make it more interesting.

When you are describing a place or a setting, it is important to bring it alive for the reader. You can do this by using your senses: sight, smell, touch, taste (although this is often tricky) and hearing.

Imagine you are describing the jungle Savitri can see from the palace:

- What can you see? You can see the plants and the animals moving through the trees.
- What can you smell? You can smell the scent of flowers and leaves.
- What can you touch? You can feel the breeze and the rain.
- What can you taste? You can taste the guava.
- What can you hear? You can hear the parrots and the leaves.

Now think of some jungle adjectives. For example:

- Colours: emerald, scarlet, azure
- Weather: humid, sweltering, scorching
- Trees: verdant, luscious, flourishing
- Animals: playful, dangerous, regal

When you plan your description, think of different parts of the jungle that you can describe and these will become your paragraphs. For example:

- Paragraph 1: Trees, leaves and sky
- Paragraph 2: Animals
- Paragraph 3: Sounds of the forest

You might begin your description like this:

> Hundreds of trees stand tall like soldiers. Their luscious green leaves provide shade, protecting its creatures from the blazing hot sun. The azure blue sky peeks through the leafy canopy, with candyfloss clouds floating gently above the horizon. On the forest floor, the leaves rustle and crackle and the moist, warm soil squelches under your feet.

Now try writing descriptions of these places. Don't forget to use lots of interesting adjectives and adverbs.

31 Write a description based on this picture of a hot, dry desert.

32 Write a description of a busy city centre.

33 Write a description of a hot, wet rainforest.

34 Write a description of a windy, rainy clifftop or mountain.

Mystery and magic

Children's libraries are full of magical tales of witches and wizards, from *The Worst Witch* to *Harry Potter*. These stories transport you to another world and use invented and mysterious language to help you imagine what it would be like to cast a spell or make friends with a wizard. You can use the same mysterious vocabulary when you write your own fantasy poems.

Skill focus: Author's use of language

In this chapter you will learn how to answer questions that ask you about the words and phrases authors use. You will have to think about how particular words fit into a passage, why they are good choices and what they tell the reader. You will also see that each question has a certain number of marks available and will learn how to make sure you get all of those marks. Don't forget that choosing words carefully in your writing is essential as well.

A reading list of books about mystery and magic and how to do your own magic tricks can be found in *English Year 3 Answers*.

➔ Comprehension

When authors write stories or poems, they choose words carefully so that the reader can really understand what they are writing about. Thinking carefully about the words and phrases used in a passage will help you to understand it better, making it more enjoyable to read. For example, a character who 'creeps' into a room sounds very different from a character who 'prances' into a room. The first sounds mysterious, the second sounds happy and excited.

Questions that ask you to think about language might look like this:

- Find a word or phrase that shows ...
- Why do you think the author chose the word/phrase ...?
- Which words show that ...?
- What does the word '...' tell you about the character/place where the story happens?

Here is a passage of text with some examples of questions:

As the castle gates creaked open, Callum looked around. The air was thick with mist and he was almost shivering in the cold. He tiptoed forward nervously and crossed the threshold. A bat suddenly swooped towards him, almost knocking his glasses off. He nearly fell over, but managed to steady himself. 'H-h-h-hello …' His voice quivered as he called out. The words just echoed back at him. There was nothing for it. He would have to investigate further. He inched towards the next door he could see. It was open only a crack but a strange green light was coming from behind the wood. With trembling hands, he pushed the door gently and it gave way at his touch. As the room behind came into view it was dark, apart from a huge cauldron in the centre, bubbling and smoking, giving out more green light. At first he thought he was alone but as his eyes adjusted to the darkness, he saw a tall, slim, cloaked figure, huddled over the cauldron, whispering words that he could just make out but could not understand.

1 'The air was thick with mist'. Why do you think the author describes the air in this way? (2 marks)

Think about the important word: thick. How do you imagine the air when you think of it being thick? Is it harder to see? Is it difficult to walk through? Your answer might look like this:

The author uses this phrase because it makes the scene feel more misty (1 mark). They do this because they want the setting to seem more spooky and mysterious (1 mark). The question is worth 2 marks so you need to give two reasons.

2 Find two words or phrases that make the place where the story happens (sometimes called the setting) seem spooky. (2 marks)

Think about what makes something seem spooky; for example, the dark, strange noises, suspicious people. Look for examples of these things in the text. Several have been highlighted for you in yellow. The question asks for two words or phrases and is worth 2 marks. There is 1 mark for each word or phrase you give.

3 'H-h-h-hello ...' What does the way the author writes this tell you about Callum? (1 mark)

Think about what this would sound like out loud and why Callum might be speaking like this. There is only 1 mark, so you only need to give one idea.

4 Find two words or phrases that the author uses to show that Callum is scared. (2 marks)

Look for words and phrases that you associate with being frightened.

Now try to answer these questions yourself.

Complete this comprehension exercise, using the guidance given above to help you answer the questions. The questions about the author's use of language are in bold.

A witch's song

Have you ever met nastier witches than these? And what a strange way of talking they have.

'Down with children! Do them in!
Boil their bones and fry their skin!
Bish them, sqvish them, bash them, mash them!
Brrreak them, shake them, slash them, smash them!
5   Offer chocs with magic powder!
Say "Eat up!" then say it louder.
Crrram them full of sticky eats,
Send them home still guzzling sveets.
And in the morning little fools
10 Go marching off to separate schools.
A girl feels sick and goes all pale.

She yells, "Hey look! I've grrrown a tail!"
A boy who's standing next to her
Screams, "Help! I think I'm growing fur!"
15 Another shouts, "Vee look like frrreaks!
There's viskers growing on our cheeks!"
A boy who vos extremely tall
Cries out, "Vot's wrong? I'm grrrowing small!"
Four tiny legs begin to sprrrout
20 From everybody rrround about.
And all at vunce, all in a trrrice,
There are no children! Only MICE!
In every school is mice galore
All rrrunning rrround the school-rrroom floor!
25 And all the poor demented teachers
Is yelling, "Hey, who are these crrreatures?"
They stand upon the desks and shout,
"Get out, you filthy mice! Get out!
Vill someone fetch some mouse-trrraps, please!
30 And don't forrrget to bring the cheese!"
Now mouse-trrraps come and every trrrap
Goes *snippy-snip* and *snappy-snap*.
The mouse-trrraps have a powerful spring,
The springs go *crack* and *snap* and *ping*!
35 Is lovely noise for us to hear!
Is music to a vitch's ear!
Dead mice is every place arrround,
Piled two feet deep upon the grrround,
Vith teachers searching left and rrright,
40 But not a single child in sight!
The teachers cry, "Vot's going on?
Oh vhere have all the children gone?
Is half-past nine and as a rrrule
They're never late as this for school!"
45 Poor teachers don't know vot to do.
Some sit and rrread, and just a few
Amuse themselves throughout the day
By sveeping all the mice avay.
AND ALL US VITCHES SHOUT HOORAY!'

From *The Witches* by Roald Dahl

29

5 What do the witches give to children to turn them into mice? (1 mark)

6 Do the teachers like the mice? How do you know? (2 marks)

7 Some of the words the witches say are spelled unusually. For example, 'will' is spelled 'vill' and 'break' is spelled 'brrreak'. Why do you think the author does this? (2 marks)

8 Find three words or phrases that show how nasty the witches are. (3 marks)

9 'The springs go *crack* and *snap* and *ping*!' Why do you think the author uses these particular words? (2 marks)

10 Why do you think the last line of the poem is in capital letters? (1 mark)

11 What is your opinion of the witches now that you have read the poem? Give a reason for your answer. (2 marks)

12 There is a rhyming pattern in this poem. Describe it in your own words. (2 marks)

Speaking and listening

13 Working in a small group, practise reading 'A witch's song' aloud and learning a few lines each off by heart. Try to put some interesting actions to the poem, and remember to use lots of expression when you perform it.

Now try the following comprehension exercise. Don't forget to think about the particular words and phrases that the author has chosen.

Choosing your dragon

Ten boys, including Hiccup who is known for being useless, are being taken on their Dragon Initiation Program by Gobber the Belch. They are hoping to become members of the Hairy Hooligan tribe and they are about to embark on the first part of the initiation: catching their dragon.

Gobber spat solemnly into the snow.

'There are three parts to the Dragon Initiation Test. The first and most dangerous part is a test of your
5 courage and skill at burglary. If you wish to enter the Hairy Hooligan Tribe, you must first catch your dragon. And that is WHY,' continued Gobber, at full volume, 'I have brought
10 you to this scenic spot. Take a look at Wild Dragon Cliff itself.'

The ten boys tipped their heads backward. The cliff loomed dizzyingly high above them, black and sinister. In summer you could barely even see the cliff as dragons of all shapes and sizes swarmed over it, snapping and biting and sending up a
15 cacophony of noise that could be heard all over Berk. But in winter the dragons were hibernating and the cliff fell silent, except for the ominous, low rumble of their snores. Hiccup could feel the vibrations through his sandals.

'Now,' said Gobber, 'do you notice those four caves about halfway up the cliff, grouped roughly in the shape of a skull?' The boys nodded. 'Inside the cave that would be
20 the right eye of the skull is the Dragon Nursery, where there are, AT THIS VERY MOMENT, three thousand young dragons having their last few weeks of winter sleep.'

'OOOOOOOH,' muttered the boys excitedly.

Hiccup swallowed hard. He happened to know considerably more about dragons than anybody else there. Ever since he was a small boy, he'd been fascinated by the creatures.
25 He'd spent hour after long hour dragon-watching in secret. (Dragon-spotters were thought to be geeks and nerds, hence the need for secrecy.) And what Hiccup had learned about dragons told him that walking into a cave with three thousand dragons in it was an act of madness. No one else seemed too concerned, however.

'In a few minutes I want you to take one of these baskets and start climbing the cliff,'
30 commanded Gobber the Belch. 'Once you are at the cave entrance, you are on your own. I am too large to squeeze my way into the tunnels that lead to the Dragon Nursery. You will enter the cave QUIETLY – and that means you too, Wartihog, unless

you want to become the first spring meal for three thousand hungry dragons, HA HA HAHA!' Gobber laughed heartily at his little joke, then continued. 'Dragons this
35 size are normally fairly harmless to man, but in these numbers they will set upon you like piranhas. There'd be nothing left of even a fatso like you, Wartihog – just a pile of bones and your helmet. HA HA HA HA! So ... you will walk QUIETLY through the cave and each boy will steal ONE sleeping dragon. Lift the dragon GENTLY from the rock and place it in your basket. Any questions so far?' Nobody had any questions.
40 'In the unlikely event that you DO wake the dragons – and you would have to be IDIOTICALLY STUPID to do so – run like thunder for the entrance to the cave. Dragons do not like cold weather and the snow will probably stop them in their tracks.'

From *How to Train Your Dragon* by Cressida Cowell

14 Find two groups of words that the author uses to show how dangerous Wild Dragon Cliff is. (2 marks)

15 Why is Hiccup more worried about going into the cave than everybody else? (1 mark)

16 Explain in your own words the difference between Wild Dragon Cliff in the summer and in the winter. (2 marks)

17 'in these numbers, they will set upon you like piranhas'. Why do you think the author compares the dragons to piranhas? (2 marks)

18 Why do you think several of Gobber's words are in capital letters? (1 mark)

19 What do you think the author means by 'run like thunder'? (2 marks)

Speaking and listening

20 Find a partner. One person chooses a word from the list below and the other person has to think of as many words that rhyme with it as they can. Now swap over. Who made the longest list of rhyming words?

spell   fire   fly   hat   wing

→ Grammar

In this section you will learn how to join short sentences together using conjunctions (joining words).

Conjunctions

To avoid using lots of simple, short sentences, you can use conjunctions to join ideas together.

Some conjunctions join ideas that are equally important. For example:

The boys captured their dragons **and** they learned how to fly them.

Would you prefer to enter the cave **or** would you like to go home?

He wanted to catch a dragon **but** he was too frightened.

Some conjunctions join ideas when one is more important than the other. For example:

Gobber took the boys to Wild Dragon Cliff **because** they needed to catch dragons.

Hiccup was scared **when** he realised he had to go into the cave.

Here are some more conjunctions you might use:

so   while   after   before

---

21 Copy out these sentences, choosing the correct conjunction from the options provided:

(a) Hiccup knew a lot about dragons when/because/so he knew how dangerous they were.

(b) The cliff was quiet because/and/or the dragons were sleeping.

(c) If the dragons wake up the boys should run and/or/so they will be eaten.

(d) The teachers screamed when/so/and the children turned into mice.

(e) The mouse traps were set so/because/after the mice would be caught.

22 For each conjunction, write a sentence containing it. Try to link the sentences to the witches or dragons you have read about.

(a) and   (d) because

(b) but   (e) while

(c) so

→ Punctuation

Exclamation marks are used to help things stand out.

Exclamation marks

Exclamation marks are used at the end of sentences instead of a full stop:

- to show strong feelings, such as excitement, anger or fear
- to show that something is being shouted or emphasised
- when people say single word sentences, such as 'wow' or 'ouch'.

For example:

'Be quiet!' yelled Gobber angrily.

Ouch! That hurt!

A boy who's standing next to her screams, 'Help! I think I'm growing fur!'

He couldn't believe his eyes, 'It's amazing!' he gasped.

You should only ever use one exclamation mark at a time.

---

23 Copy out these sentences and decide if they need an exclamation mark or not.

   (a) Hiccup looked anxiously at the sleeping dragons.

   (b) He called to the others, 'Watch out.'

   (c) Help.

   (d) It's a miracle.

   (e) Gobber laughed at the terrified boys.

→ Spelling

Some words have letters in them that you can't hear when you say the word out loud. These are called silent letters. Often they come at the beginning of the word. For example:

write: you can't hear the w

gnome: you can't hear the g

knock: you can't hear the k

Sometimes the silent letter is somewhere else in the word. For example:

comb: you can't hear the b

where: you can't hear the h

island: you can't hear the s

---

24 Write out these words and write the silent letter in a different colour.

    (a) knobbly   **(d)** thumb   **(g)** wrap

    (b) white   **(e)** knot

    (c) listen   **(f)** know

25 Now use these words in a sentence. Try to link the sentences to the witches or dragons you have read about.

    (a) knees   **(c)** gnaw   **(e)** whether

    (b) climb   **(d)** castle

➔ Vocabulary

When you are describing something, you might want to compare it to other things. For example:

Hiccup was the **cleverest** of the boys   Cleverest means the most clever.

All dragons are scary but this one was
the **scariest**.   Scariest means the most scary.

These comparing words are called superlatives.

Usually, you create superlatives by adding -est to an adjective: tall + est = tallest.

If the adjective ends in -e, just add -st: brave + est = bravest

If the adjective ends in -y, take it off and add -iest: silly + est = silliest

If the adjective has more than two syllables, just add the word 'most' before it: beautiful = most beautiful

26 Make superlatives from these adjectives.

　(a) small　**(b)** high　**(c)** simple　**(d)** easy　**(e)** difficult

27 Now use each of the superlatives you have made in a sentence.

Speaking and listening

28 Sit in a circle with your classmates. Begin narrating a ghost story, taking it in turns to make up the next line of the story. You could begin with these lines: *Suddenly the great oak door behind us slammed shut, plunging the room into darkness. I knew we should never have come …*

→ Writing

In this section you are going to write a poem like 'The witch's song', which you read earlier. Think back to that poem and what made it exciting to read. You could use some of these ideas in your own writing.

Before you start writing a poem, think about the following questions:

- What is your poem about?
- Will it tell a story or just describe something?
- Will it rhyme? If so, which lines will rhyme?

Once you have thought about these questions, poetry is about experimenting. Try things out, read them aloud, change things, improve things and add things until you are happy with your poem. Don't be afraid to cross things out and start again.

Imagine you are writing a poem about witches casting a spell. First answer the questions above:

- The poem is about a witch's spell.
- It is going to list the ingredients of the spell and what the spell does.

- Pairs of lines will rhyme.
- Some rhyming words are:

witch/stitch	smoke/spoke/folk	wing/sing
pot/hot/not	frog/bog	all/small

Now it is time to try to write your poem. Remember, you will probably change lots of things as you go along and that's fine. Try to keep the story or subject of your poem in your mind at all times. This will make it more effective. You might start like this:

Very hard to find a rhyme for 'cauldron'. 'Pot' is much easier.

'Stands' was quite boring. 'Stirs' fits better with the idea of the cauldron.

Standing round the iron ~~cauldron~~ pot,
The air is misty, dark and ~~hot.~~
One witch ~~stands~~ stirs and one witch sings,
Their black cloaks flutter like bats' wings.

Spells to punish, spells to mend,
Spells to send you round the bend,
Spells to make you ~~fat or thin~~ thin or fat,
To give you whiskers like a cat.

~~The witches know all of these spells,~~ These spells, the witches know them all,
Words to make you shrink so small,
Spells that make you disappear,
Spells that you should ever fear.

You'll vanish in a puff of smoke,
Once these magic words are spoke,

This sentence has been rewritten in a different order to help find a rhyme.

These words have been switched around to help find a rhyme on the next line.

This should really be 'spoken' but in a poem you can play with grammar a bit. Witches probably don't speak like we do so it's okay to do this for a rhyme.

Notice where words and ideas have changed as the poem has been written.

Now try these activities, using what you have learnt.

29 Write a poem about witches or wizards casting spells.

30 Write a poem about a magician putting on a magic show. Think of the different tricks he or she might do and the words they might use while performing.

31 Write a poem about a dragon. It could just describe the dragon or it could tell a story about a dragon.

32 Write a poem about making a wish. Think of things people do when they wish: close their eyes, cross their fingers, keep it secret.

Treasure seekers

Is there anything more exciting than the idea of finding some buried treasure? You are about to read about some real and imagined hunts for precious hidden treasures. These texts are full of mystery and suspense and encourage you to put yourself in the shoes of the treasure seekers. As you are reading, imagine what they must be thinking and feeling.

Skill focus: Purpose and structure

In this section you will look at the way different types of texts are structured and the different features they have. You will learn that the purpose of a text influences how it is structured. It is also very useful to think about these things when you are planning your own writing.

A reading list of books about pirates can be found in *English Year 3 Answers.*

➔ Comprehension

Different types of texts are structured differently. This is because they have different purposes; they are written for different reasons. If you understand why a text has been written, it is easier to see why it has a particular structure. Look at the list below:

- Stories are written to entertain people.
- Information texts are written to teach people facts about a subject.
- Newspapers are written to tell people about what is happening in the world.
- Poems are written to entertain people and to make people think about things in a different way.
- Instructions are written to tell people how to do or make something.
- Persuasive texts are written to convince people to believe in something or do something.

Have a look at the text below:

Multiple blue lights flashed on the control panel in front of Flight Commander Collins. The accelerator booster nodes were losing power; he would have to initiate the emergency sequence. Although Genesis VI was the most advanced spacecraft of the 35th century, it was not without its faults. The meteor storm the previous night had damaged the navigation sensors and now the craft was rotating too fast for comfort. As the most senior officer, Collins had to make the call.

He switched on the announcement system.

'Attention! All crew, report to the navigation deck immediately. This is a Code Blue. I repeat, Code Blue. Respiration apparatus and full protective suits should be worn.'

Ahead of him, through the vast curved window, was total blackness. He could feel the ship spinning but he could see nothing to focus on. Just wide open space. The universe; ready to be explored.

1 Which of the following types of story best describes the passage you have read? (1 mark)

science fiction   adventure fiction   humorous fiction

Think about the text. What did you read that might give you a clue as to the type of story it is? Did it make you laugh? Where was it set? Were there any particular words, characters or actions that you usually find in a particular type of story?

2 How can you tell it belongs to this type of story? Give two examples from the text. (2 marks)

Use the ideas you've already come up with to help you. Some have been highlighted in the text. Remember that for 2 marks you should give two examples, as the question instructs.

3 Do you think this extract comes from the beginning, the middle or the end of the story? Give a reason for your answer. (2 marks)

Think about what you have read. Does it seem like something has already happened or something is about to happen? Do you feel like you have started reading half way through the story? There are 2 marks available here, 1 for identifying the correct part of the story and the other for your reason.

Now try to answer the questions yourself.

In non-fiction texts, you might be asked about more obvious things such as:

- Why has the author used subheadings?
- Why are the steps in the instructions numbered?
- Why has the author included pictures with labels?
- What is the purpose of the information in the box at the top?

Again, think about why the text has been written to help you to work out why the features you are being asked about have been included. For example, the information above has been presented in bullet points to make each individual idea stand out.

Now try this comprehension exercise, using the simple steps above to help you answer the questions. Questions about purpose and structure are in bold.

Buried treasure

Long John Silver and his band of ruthless pirates are searching for buried treasure. Young Jim Hawkins, the hero of this story, is with them. But Dr Livesey and Ben Gunn are on their trail.

The map said Flint's chest was buried under a tall tree in the shadow of Spyglass Hill. As we neared the spot marked 'X' on the map, a pirate up ahead began to shout. But he hadn't found treasure … He'd found a skeleton.

In the silence that followed, a spine-chilling voice filled the air. It sang a sailor's song.
5   'The ghost of Captain Flint!' cried the pirates.

'Don't be stupid,' said Long John. 'It's just someone trying to scare us.'

Another pirate spotted a tall tree and everyone charged over to it. But at the bottom of the tree was an empty hole. The treasure had gone.

Long John tapped me on my good shoulder. 'There's going to be trouble,' he
10   whispered. Was he on our side now?

I clutched my pistols tightly, feeling sweat run down my neck.

The pirates stared at Long John menacingly and drew their guns. Just then, shots rang out. Dr Livesey and Ben Gunn charged out of the bushes with a sailor named Gray. The terrified pirates ran off.

15 'Quick!' said the doctor. 'We must get to the boats before the pirates.' We sprinted out to the beach, with Long John hobbling behind.

'Don't leave me!' he panted. 'The others will kill me.'

We clambered aboard a boat and rowed for the Hispaniola.

From Robert Louis Stevenson's *Treasure Island*, retold by Angela Wilkes

---

4 **Which of the following best describes the type of story this passage belongs to? (1 mark)**

   science fiction   instructions   adventure   myth

5 **Find two words or phrases that show it belongs to this type of story. (2 marks)**

6 **'...feeling sweat run down my neck.' What does this tell us about the person telling the story? (1 mark)**

7 **Why has the author used speech in the story? (1 mark)**

8 **Why do you think Long John Silver thought there would be trouble? (1 mark)**

9 **How did Dr Livesey and Ben Gunn frighten away the pirates? (2 marks)**

10 **Do you think this passage comes from the beginning, the middle or the end of the book it was taken from? Give a reason for your answer. (2 marks)**

Speaking and listening

11 Play the Pirate Name word game. Think up a pirate character and then give them a name that includes their characteristics. For example, Captain Dashing Dagger or Limping Longbeard Lenny. Now act out or draw what your pirate looks like.

Try this comprehension exercise. It is a different type of text, which was written for a different purpose and therefore has a different structure.

How to make a treasure map

In stories, old maps of desert islands help people find buried treasure. Make your own treasure map for a fantasy island.

You will need:

- Paper
- Poster paints
- Paintbrush
5 - Pencil
- Ruler
- Felt-tip pens

1 Scrunch a piece of paper into a loose ball. Then flatten it out
10 with your hands.

2 Dilute some green or brown paint to make it very watery. Paint a wash over the whole sheet of crumpled paper. Leave to dry.

15 3 Draw a grid of squares over the paper with a pencil and ruler. Each line should be the same distance apart.

4 Draw the outline of a desert island using felt-tips pens. Make it an interesting, unusual shape. Add some waves to show where the sea is.

5 Draw some pictures on your map to stand for different things, such as lakes and
20 volcanoes. Make the symbols small and simple.

6 Draw a key to explain your symbols and add a north arrow. Shade the edges to make the map look old.

Slightly adapted from *Maps and Mapping* by Deborah Chancellor

43

12 Why is the list of things you will need at the beginning of the passage? (1 mark)

13 Why has the author used bullet points for the things you will need? (1 mark)

14 Why do you think you have to 'Scrunch a piece of paper'? (1 mark)

15 What do you think the purpose of the 'grid of squares' is? (1 mark)

16 Why are the instructions numbered? (1 mark)

17 If you could add a seventh instruction to make the map even better, what would it be? (2 marks)

Speaking and listening

18 Think again about how instructions are put together. Look back at the example of how to make a treasure map. Think about the numbered tasks, each one beginning with a verb (doing word). Choose a simple task, like brushing your teeth, tying your shoelaces or riding your bike. Then imagine you had to instruct someone how to do this task using **spoken** words, rather than writing it down. Try it out with a friend.

→ Grammar

When you are using a map, you need to know which direction to go in and where things are. The words we use for this are called prepositions.

Prepositions

Prepositions are words of direction or position (you can remember this because there is a clue in the word itself: pre**position**). In a sentence, they are found before a noun. For example:

The pirates put the gold coins **in** their pockets.

Draw a grid **on** the paper.

Here are some more common prepositions:

| with | over | in | through | above | below | under |
| at | between | to | into | from | off | underneath |

---

19 Copy out these sentences and underline the prepositions:

(a) The treasure was buried beneath a tall tree.

(b) The pirates stared at the skeleton.

(c) The pirates jumped into the hole.

(d) A sound came from the bushes.

(e) Draw a grid over the map.

20 Copy and complete these sentences, adding in suitable prepositions from the list above:

(a) They walked _____ the forest.

(b) Nothing stood _____ the pirates and the treasure.

(c) The treasure was buried _____ the ground.

(d) They couldn't escape _____ the island.

(e) A bird flew _____ their heads and landed in a tree.

➲ Punctuation

It is important to separate items in a list with commas.

Commas in lists

Whenever you list something, you need to use commas to separate the things in the list. You use the word 'and' to separate the last two items in the list. For example:

You will need paper, paint, scissors **and** a ruler.

The pirates were terrifying, loud, scruffy **and** dangerous.

21 Copy out these sentences and add the missing commas:

   (a) On the island there were mountains rivers lakes and beaches.

   (b) The pirates had muskets swords daggers and pistols.

   (c) In the treasure chest they found gold silver rubies diamonds and emeralds.

   (d) The water was blue calm and deep.

   (e) To make a treasure map you will need to draw paint cut and paste.

22 Turn these lists into full sentences by adding extra words and punctuation:

   (a) parrots monkeys dolphins snakes

   (b) north south east west

   (c) brave clever handsome

   (d) cliffs streams caves forest

   (e) walk climb search dig

➔ Spelling

In this section you will learn to spell words that end in -ture and -sure.

The 'zher' sound in words like **treasure** is always spelled -sure.

   For example: mea**sure**

The 'tcher' sound in words like furni**ture** is spelled -ture, unless the word comes from a word that ends in -tch and then it is spelled -tcher.

   For example: na**ture**

   But: ca**tcher**, because the root word is ca**tch**

23 Write sentences using each of these words:

(a) pleasure   (c) picture   (e) leisure

(b) creature   (d) adventure

24 Copy out these sentences and correct the spelling mistakes:

(a) The animals at the zoo were kept in large enclozures.

(b) The cyclist went home when she got a punctcher.

(c) The pirates will captcher the captain.

(d) If we find the treazure, will we have a rich futcher.

(e) The sculptcher was made of stone.

➲ Vocabulary

In adventure stories, there is often a good character and a bad character. We might call them the hero and the villain. Here are some words to describe good and bad characters:

evil	virtuous	villainous	spiteful	honourable	wicked
noble	honest	diabolical	righteous	truthful	benevolent

25 Sort the words above into two groups: one for words used to describe good characters and one for words used to describe bad characters. Use a dictionary to help you if you need to.

26 Now write three sentences using some of these words.

Speaking and listening

27 Working in small groups, act out the scene from 'Buried treasure' when Long John Silver and his pirates find that the treasure has gone. What happens next? Perform your scene for the class. Think particularly about the expressions on the pirates' faces and the tone of the pirates' voices.

⊙ Writing

In this section, you are going to write some instructions. Think about their purpose, as you did in the comprehension section earlier. We give instructions to teach somebody how to do or make something, so they need to be broken down into small steps and be helpful and clear. Instructions need to include the following things:

- A title explaining what the instructions are for.

- A list of things you will need. This should come first.

- A list of actions to take, with each action in the list describing one small step in the process you are describing.

- Each action should be written in a sentence that starts with a verb (doing word). For example, 'Draw a line' *not* 'You draw a line'.

- The instructions should be numbered or begin with words that give them an order such as 'first', 'next' and 'then'.

- If it would help the person using the instructions, you could include a diagram or picture.

Here is an example. Imagine you are writing instructions for how to be a good pirate.

How to be a pirate

You will need:

- A pirate hat

- A cutlass

- A parrot

- An eyepatch

First, put on your pirate hat.

Next, tuck your cutlass into your belt. Practise pulling it out quickly to fend off your enemies.

Now, put your parrot on your shoulder. Teach it to say 'Pieces of eight' or other pirate phrases.

Then, put your eyepatch on. Be careful when you walk around with it on, especially if you are near the edge of the ship.

Finally, say, 'Arrrrrggh,' very loudly.

You are now a pirate!

Try writing some instructions yourself. Use the steps above to help you.

28 Imagine you are preparing for a camping trip. Write instructions for setting up camp.

29 Write instructions for making or building something. It could be a Lego™ house, a model airplane or a cardboard castle. Whatever you like!

30 Write instructions for something you have to do at school. It could be drawing a graph in Maths, playing a musical instrument or scoring a goal in football.

31 Write a recipe for a good friendship. Think about what you can do to be the best friend possible.

Sky full of stars

The night sky is a wonderful sight. It is full of stars, planets and possibilities. People have explored a small part of space but there is so much more to learn about it, which makes it both exciting to read about and great to write about. You only need to look up after dark to find your inspiration. What do you think is out there?

Skill focus: Joining the dots

In this section you will have a chance to practise all the different skills you have already learnt: retrieval, inference, author's use of language, purpose and structure, and matching your answer to the number of marks available.

A reading list of books about space, astronauts, space travel and the universe can be found in *English Year 3 Answers*.

➲ Comprehension

Here are a few top tips to help you:

- Remember to look carefully at the questions and identify the key words.

- Scan the text for the key words and ideas in order to find the answer.

- If the answer isn't instantly obvious, look for clues, related pieces of information that might help you to work out the answer (infer the answer).

- Think about why the text was written and what features it has to make it useful/interesting/clear for the reader.

- Look at the number of marks the question is worth, and write enough to get all of the marks.

Here is your first comprehension exercise. It is a poem. Use the tips above and what you have learnt in Chapters 1 to 4 to help you answer the questions.

Silvery moon

> In this poem, the poet is describing the moon that he sees at midnight. He feels as though it is looking at him, protecting him.

    I dreamed of monsters late last night
    And woke to find my room was light;
    Not sunshine bright as in the day,
    But gently shining where I lay.

5   To my window then I crept,
    While the household quietly slept.
    I softly drew the curtains wide
    And stood up tall to peek outside.

    A vision in a window frame!
10   Familiar – and yet not the same.
    The lawn spread smoothly down below
    And shimmered in a glimm'ring glow.

    Beneath the oak tree's friendly shade,
    Silvery shadows ran and played;
15   The holly bush stood, sparkly, stark,
    Prickly glittering, light and dark.

    This homely plot I know so well,
    Now captured in this magic spell;
    This special change in all I see;
20   What can this mean, how can this be?

    And in my questing, wondering why?
    I raise my eyes up to the sky,
    Where rides the moon, its friendly face
    Smiling down through boundless space.

25   Why, there's the answer – Man's Old Friend,
    Whose silken rays our troubles mend.
    His kindly presence fills my head.
    Monsters banished – back to bed!

By Alan Hammond

1 What did the poet dream of last night? (1 mark)

2 When did the poet wake up? How do you know? (2 marks)

3 Why do you think the word 'glimm'ring' (line 12) is spelled in this unusual way? (1 mark)

4 What had cast a 'magic spell' on the garden? (1 mark)

5 Find and copy three examples of words or phrases that describe the light from the moon. (3 marks)

6 Why might the poet think that the moon has a 'friendly face'? Give two ideas. (2 marks)

7 Can you spot a rhyming pattern in this poem? Describe it in your own words. (1 mark)

8 How do you think the poet feels at the end of the poem? Give a reason for your answer. (2 marks)

Speaking and listening

9 Prepare a performance of the poem 'Silvery moon' with a partner or in a small group. Think about how to express the meaning of the poem and the different feelings that the poet has. Try to learn the words by heart, if you can, to help you perform it well.

Now try this comprehension exercise. It is a non-fiction text and you will find different types of questions to practise.

A giant leap for mankind

This passage recounts the historic moment when Neil Armstrong first stood on the Moon in 1969.

On 20th July, 1969, Neil Armstrong clambered down the ladder of the lunar module *Eagle* and became the first human being to stand on the surface of the Moon. The History News gave a glowing report of this monumental milestone in the history of space exploration …

One-fifth of the entire population of the world watched TV in wonder as American
5 astronaut Neil Armstrong stepped on to the surface of the Moon.

'That's one small step for a man, one giant leap for mankind,' his voice echoed
round mission control at Houston, Texas, 384 000 kilometres away.

A few seconds later, Armstrong was joined on the surface by Edwin 'Buzz' Aldrin.
The third member of the crew, Michael Collins, was still in orbit around the Moon.
10 He had remained in *Apollo 11's* command module *Columbia*.

The three men left Earth in their space capsule *Apollo 11* on 16th July, thrust into
space by its awesomely powerful *Saturn 5* rocket.

It was around noon four days later when Armstrong and Aldrin first crawled into
the *Apollo* lunar module – the *Eagle* – to begin the descent procedure. Half an hour
15 later, Collins pressed the button that
released the *Eagle* from *Columbia* and
sent it on its way down to the Moon.
Minutes later, Armstrong told mission
control, 'The *Eagle* has landed.' The
20 answer from mission control was a
huge sigh of relief, and a message
went back to the Moon saying, 'We're
breathing again. Thanks a lot.'

Armstong's next task was to pull a cord
25 on the *Eagle* and lower a live television
camera. A few minutes later, 600
million people watched him take his
historic steps.

From *The History News: In Space* by Michael
Johnstone

■ Neil Armstrong standing on the surface of
the Moon

10 What nationality is Neil Armstrong? (1 mark)

11 'That's one small step for a man, one giant leap for mankind.' What do
you think Neil Armstrong meant when he said this? (2 marks)

12 How did the people at mission control feel once they knew the *Eagle*
had landed on the Moon? Copy something from the text to support
your answer. (2 marks)

13 How were people around the world able to watch a man walk on the Moon for the first time? (1 mark)

14 Why do you think this passage contains so many numbers (figures)? (2 mark)

15 What is the purpose of the first paragraph of this passage? (1 mark)

16 Why has the author used the word 'historic' to describe Armstrong's steps on the Moon? (2 marks)

Speaking and listening

17 With a friend, prepare and perform a short interview in which one of you is Neil Armstrong and the other plays the part of a television interviewer. Imagine that this is Armstrong's first interview since his historic mission to the Moon.

→ Grammar

In this section you will practise the topics you have learnt about already in previous chapters: nouns, adjectives, adverbs, conjunctions and prepositions.

18 Copy out this passage. Underline the nouns and add an interesting adjective to each noun.

As the day ends, people climb into their beds. Birds fly to their nests. The sun disappears and the sky gets dark. High in the sky, the Moon shines brightly. The stars twinkle like diamonds.

19 Copy and complete these sentences, adding in appropriate prepositions:

(a) The crew flew _____ the Moon in *Columbia*.

(b) The lunar module was released _____ the main command module.

(c) Stars glitter _____ in the sky.

(d) Aldrin went _____ the Moon _____ Armstrong but Collins stayed _____ the command module.

(e) When the Moon passes _____ of the Sun, it is called an eclipse.

(f) The Earth travels _____ the Sun.

20 Copy this passage, adding adverbs to some of the verbs to make it more interesting:

Sam fell asleep. He had worked all day and was exhausted. As he drifted off, he began to dream. His dreams were exciting. He found himself racing cars, climbing mountains, swimming with sharks and playing football in the cup final. When he woke up he was smiling. What a brilliant night!

21 Copy and complete these sentences, adding in appropriate conjunctions:

(a) Mission control was pleased _____ the lunar module landed safely.

(b) Two men went to the Moon _____ one stayed on the spacecraft.

(c) We can't see the Moon in the day _____ it is still in the sky.

(d) Sometimes it feels like the Moon is watching you _____ you are sleeping.

(e) Would you rather travel to the Moon _____ another planet?

➲ Punctuation

Here you will revise capital letters, full stops, exclamation marks, apostrophes and commas.

22 Copy out this passage, adding in the missing full stops, capital letters and exclamation marks:

Wow one day we might all be visiting the Moon for our holidays spacecraft are being developed for tourist trips to the Moon and possibly other planets you could go to outer space rather than going to spain or france for your summer break that's incredible you could write a great postcard from the Moon you could stay in a cosmic hotel and at night you would look up and see earth in the sky

23 Copy out these sentences, adding in the missing apostrophes:

(a) I wouldnt like to go to the Moon.

(b) It isnt surprising that Neil Armstrong is so famous.

(c) Dont forget to look at the stars.

(d) I wasnt awake late enough to see the Moon appear.

(e) Ive got a huge telescope for watching the night sky.

24 Now write out the sentences in question 23 again, replacing the contractions with complete words.

25 Copy out these sentences, adding the missing commas in the lists:

(a) When I am older I would like to be an astronaut a doctor a fireman a policeman or a teacher.

(b) If I were an astronaut I would like to float without gravity wear a spacesuit fly at high speed and explore new planets.

(c) Astronauts have to be clever healthy fit and brave.

(d) The night sky is black velvety beautiful and scattered with stars.

(e) Before I go to bed I brush my teeth read my book turn out the light and look at the stars.

➲ Spelling

Now it is time to practise the spelling rules you have learnt in Chapters 1 to 4.

26 Copy and complete these phrases, adding in the missing words. For example: one planet, two planets.

(a) one astronaut, two _____   **(d)** one galaxy, two _____

(b) one journey, two _____   **(e)** one success, two _____

(c) one discovery, two _____

27 Add -ly to these adjectives to make adverbs. Don't forget to change the spelling if you need to. Then use each adverb in a sentence.

(a) slow   **(c)** swift   **(e)** steady

(b) magical   **(d)** shaky

28 Copy out this passage, correcting the spelling mistakes. There are ten to find.

As the spaceship took off it sounded like a bom exploding. We new it would be loud but not that loud. We lisened carefully and hoped nothing would go rong. My nuckles went wite and my nees were trembling. The spaceship soared into the sky and soon the hole rocket had disappeared behind the clouds. The newspapers rote all about it the next day and I

■ The space shuttle *Discovery* launching from Kennedy Space Center in Florida

was lucky to have been there wen it happened.

29 Copy out these sentences, choosing the correct spelling from the available options:

(a) Space travel will be more normal in the fuchure/future/futcher.

(b) People think there might be living creatchers/creatures/creaters on other planets.

(c) Watching the stars gives me a lot of pleazure/pleasure/pleaser.

(d) On the Moon, the astronauts took many measurements/meazurements/measherments.

➜ Vocabulary

In this section you will revisit some of the vocabulary words you learnt in earlier chapters. You will use them in sentences to make sure you understand what they mean, and then you will find some more words.

Words of size	Verbs of movement	Superlatives	Good vs evil
baby	swoop	fastest	generous
giant	pounce	bravest	rotten
colossal	creep	funniest	wicked
tiny	slither	youngest	honourable
great	sprint	scariest	noble

30 Choose two or three words from different columns and write a sentence using them. Do this five times.

31 Now draw the table for yourself, finding new words to go into the columns. Use a thesaurus to help you.

Speaking and listening

32 In a large circle, take turns to call out an exciting adjective to describe the journey to the Moon. Think about the sights and sounds inside (and outside) the spacecraft. Then take turns to do the same for the Moon itself. Make your words as interesting as possible.

➡ Writing

Here are some activities that provide you with a chance to practise the skills you have learnt in Chapters 1 to 4. There are some things you should always do when you create a piece of writing:

- Plan what you want to write.

- When you are planning, think about why you are writing. What is the purpose of your piece of writing?

- Use capital letters and full stops.

- Choose the best adjectives and adverbs you can to make your writing interesting.

- Use paragraphs (or verses in a poem) to divide up your ideas.

- Check your work at the end for any silly mistakes.

Now try these activities. Go back to previous chapters and have another look if you can't remember what you need to do.

---

33 Write a short story with two animal characters. They could be friends or enemies. It might be set in a zoo, a hedgerow, a jungle or any other setting where the animals could live.

34 Write a description of the night sky, a sunrise or a sunset. Include lots of adjectives, adverbs and interesting verbs.

35 Write a poem that describes the Moon, the Sun, the planets or the stars.

36 Write instructions for building a cardboard rocket ship. Think of all of the different things you will need and the steps you will need to take.

Interesting insects

Insects come in all shapes and sizes. From elegant dragonflies buzzing over ponds in the summer sun to beautiful multi-coloured butterflies landing gently on a rose bush, insects are all around us, having adventures of their own. By learning about these creatures, you can include them in your stories and poems and share their beauty with others.

Skill focus: Summary

In this chapter you will learn how to summarise what you have read. This means explaining what the text, or part of the text, is about in fewer words.

A reading list of books about insects can be found in *English Year 3 Answers*.

➔ Comprehension

Sometimes when you are reading, you will notice that certain paragraphs, verses or sections concentrate on a particular topic or idea. If you can describe this in a few words, you are summarising it. We summarise all the time in life – when we're telling someone about a great film by describing the best bits, telling someone about our day at school or writing a postcard when we're on holiday. We only mention the most important things, rather than retelling every single detail.

Questions that ask you to summarise might look like this:

- Give an adjective to describe ...
- Summarise the first paragraph.
- What is the main idea in ...?
- Which word best describes ...?

To answer summary questions you need to think about what you have read as a whole. Make sure your answer makes sense for the whole passage, paragraph or verse that you are asked about. A summary should be true for everything in the passage, paragraph or verse, not just a bit of it.

Here is a text and some example questions:

> The sea is a mirror, its surface so clear,
> Still in the morning as the sun appears,
> Deep, azure blue like a warm soothing bath,
> Perfectly still like a pure pane of glass.
>
> But here comes the wind and the surface grows rough,
> The mirror-like surface is broken and scuffed,
> The angry waves rise high and then crash,
> The surf hits the rocks in an almighty splash.
>
> But when the storm calms and the water is quiet,
> The waves settle down and they call off their riot,
> The setting sun falls in one perfect motion,
> Reflecting bright colours in the smooth, glistening ocean.

1 Which word best describes the sea in the first verse? (1 mark)

     stormy   calm   deep

Reread the first verse and look at all three words above. A sea like a mirror is not 'stormy'. The word 'deep' in the verse refers to the colour, not the sea itself. 'Calm' isn't used in the verse but it does summarise how the sea looks in the whole verse. Your answer might look like this:

The word 'calm' best describes the sea in the first verse. (1 mark)

2 Choose an adjective of your own to describe the sea in the second verse. Give a reason for your answer. (2 marks)

Reread the second verse and think of some words that describe the sea, which haven't been used by the poet. Make sure the word describes the sea in the whole verse. And don't forget to choose something from that verse that backs up what you are saying and include it in your answer. The question asks you to give a reason for the word you have chosen, and you will only score 2 marks if you provide a reason as well as an adjective.

3 Summarise the idea of this poem in your own words. (2 marks)

Think about what the poet is saying about the sea. The poet notices different moods of the sea. Do you think he likes the sea or not? What does his poem tell you about the sea? For 2 marks you will need to give two ideas.

Now try to answer Questions 2 and 3 yourself.

Try this comprehension exercise, using the guidance above to help you answer the questions. Summary questions are in bold.

Good company

This poem is all about the creepy crawlies that live in houses.

I sleep in a room at the top of a house
With a flea, and a fly, and a soft-scratching mouse,
And a spider that hangs by a thread from the ceiling,
Who gives me each day such a curious feeling
5   When I watch him at work on the beautiful weave
Of his web that's so fine I can hardly believe
It won't all end up in such a terrible tangle,
For he sways as he weaves, and spins as he dangles.
I cannot get up to that spider, I know,
10 And I hope he won't get down to me here below,
And yet when I awake in the chill morning air
I'd miss him if he were not still swinging there,
For I have in my room such good company,
There's him, and the mouse, and the fly, and the flea.

'Good Company' by Leonard Clark from *Classic Poems to Read Aloud* selected by James Berry

4 With how many creatures does the poet share his room? (1 mark)

5 Where is the poet's room? (1 mark)

6 Find and copy two words or phrases that describe how the spider moves. (2 marks)

7 Describe two different feelings the poet has about the spider. Give a reason for each of your choices. (4 marks)

8 Can you think of an alternative title for this poem? Give a reason for your choice. (2 marks)

9 Would you like to live in this room? Why or why not? (2 marks)

10 Describe the rhyming pattern in this poem. (1 mark)

Speaking and listening

11 How do you react when you see a spider or a wasp? Do you stay calm or do you jump about? Working with a partner, pretend you have just seen an insect that frightens one of you. The other person remains calm and cannot understand what all the fuss is about. Perform your scene for the class.

Now try this comprehension exercise. It is a non-fiction text about different types of insects.

King of the insects

In this passage you will learn all about beetles.

Beetles

If you pick an insect at random, there is a good chance that it will be a beetle. That is because beetles are the most successful insects on Earth. So far, scientists have

identified nearly 400 000 different
5   species – some are only just visible to
    the naked eye, while others are as big
    as an adult's hand. Adult beetles have
    extra-tough bodies and strong legs, but
    their most important feature is their
10 hardened forewings, which fit over
    their hindwings like a case. With this
    special protection, they can clamber
    about in all kinds of places to search
    for food.

15 ### Gentle giant

    Weighing up to 100g (4oz) – about
    three times as much as a mouse –
    Goliath beetles are the heaviest insects
    in the world. Like most beetles, these
20 tropical monsters have hardened forewings, called elytra, which protect the more
    delicate hindwings. When a beetle flies, the elytra open up, but only the hindwings
    beat. Goliath beetles feed on forest flowers, and have small heads with stubby
    mouthparts. They have strong legs that end in hooked feet.

    ### Beetle colours

25 Many beetles are jet black, but some have eye-catching colours. The tropical leaf
    beetle, from Southeast Asia, is iridescent, with a beautiful metallic sheen. Some
    scarab beetles glisten like pieces of gold, while many smaller beetles have bright
    stripes or spots, warning predators that they are dangerous to eat. Wasp beetles have
    a bold yellow and black pattern – a colour scheme that makes other animals think
30 they can sting.

    ### Scavenging beetle

    The churchyard beetle is a typical scavenger, coming out to feed after dark. It lives on
    the dead remains of animals and plants, and also on any small live animals that come
    its way. Scavenging beetles clear up all kinds of natural waste, which helps to break
35 down nutrients, so they can be used by plants again and again. These beetles can
    cause problems if they get indoors, because some of them eat stored food.

    From *e.explore: Insect* by David Burnie

12 How many species of beetle have been found by scientists? (1 mark)

13 Why are a beetle's hardened forewings so important? (1 mark)

14 Which of the following words best describes the Goliath beetle? (1 mark)

dangerous   weighty   carnivorous

15 How do you think wasp beetles got their name? (1 mark)

16 Choose a word of your own to describe beetles. Give a reason for your answer. (2 marks)

17 Why would you not want a scavenging beetle inside your house? (1 mark)

18 Summarise what you have learnt about the colours of beetles. Write only two sentences. (2 marks)

Speaking and listening

19 Think of a few of your favourite films or books. Now find a partner and a timer. Take it in turns to summarise one of the films or books you thought of for your partner without mentioning what it is called. Can your partner guess what it is? Try summarising your first film or book in 30 seconds and your second one in 20 seconds. Can you summarise your third in 10 seconds? Can your partner still identify what it is? How about 5 seconds?

➔ Grammar

In this section you will think about the way that information texts are set out on the page and the purpose of the different features.

Headings and subheadings

When you are writing non-fiction or information texts, you can use headings and subheadings to divide up your text. These act as signposts for the reader, so that they know what each part of the text is about. This book has headings and subheadings: can you find them?

Take a look at the passage about beetles that you read earlier:

- The heading shows what the whole text is about. Headings are usually short and catchy to get the reader's attention.
- The subheadings summarise what each paragraph is about.

---

20 Read the text below and create the missing heading and four subheadings.

Heading

Subheading 1

There are many different types of ants, which live in different parts of the world and in different habitats. Although some people find them annoying, they are amazing creatures.

Subheading 2

Ants' bodies are divided into three parts. They have two stomachs, one for the food they eat and one for food they collect and share with other ants. Ants have six legs, each with a claw on the end. This means they can climb and cling onto many surfaces without falling off. Although their eyes are not very good, their antennae are excellent for sensing sounds and smells.

Subheading 3

Ants build large nests with many chambers. Each is used for a different purpose: storing food, storing waste, keeping babies safe. Many hundreds of ants live in a nest. They work together to build and increase the size of the nest, protect the young, fight off predators and collect food.

Subheading 4

Although there are many female ants in a nest, there is only one queen. She lays eggs, which the workers look after.

➔ Punctuation

In this section you will practise using question marks.

Question marks

A question mark is used, instead of a full stop, at the end of a sentence that is a question. It shows the reader that a question is being asked. It always comes at the end of the sentence.

You can see that the question mark (**?**) has a full stop at the bottom, to show it is at the end of a sentence.

You will know a sentence is a question if it can be answered. For example:

I found an earthworm under a log.   *There is no answer to this so it is not a question.*

What did you find under the log?   *You can answer this:* I found an earthworm. *It is a question.*

---

21 Copy out these sentences, adding a question mark or full stop:

(a) What is your favourite insect

(b) Are you afraid of spiders

(c) He asked me what I saw in the garden

(d) The spider web was beautiful

(e) What do flies eat for breakfast

(f) I went to the library to find out where wasps build their nests

22 Here are the answers to some questions. Work out what the questions might have been and write them down. Don't forget to include question marks.

(a) Bees are black and yellow.

(b) Insects have six legs.

(c) Butterflies live for between a week and a year.

(d) The most common insect is the beetle.

(e) Spiders eat other insects, which they catch in their webs.

➲ Spelling

In this section you will practise using prefixes that change a word to mean its opposite. A prefix is a group of letters that you add to the beginning of a word to create a new word. For example:

un + happy = **un**happy = not happy

dis + agree = **dis**agree = not agree

mis + understand = **mis**understand = not understand

The prefix in- can also mean 'not' when added to the beginning of a word, for example:

in + correct = incorrect

Depending on the spelling of the word, the prefix might change:

- Before the letter -r it becomes ir-. For example: **ir**regular
- Before the letters -m and -p, it becomes im-. For example: **im**mature and **im**possible
- Before the letter -l, it becomes il-. For example: **il**legal

---

23 Choose the correct prefix to add to these words to change the meaning to the opposite. Use a dictionary if you need to.

    mis-   dis-   un-

(a) understand	**(d)** tidy	**(g)** lucky
(b) appear	**(e)** behave	**(h)** kind
(c) obey	**(f)** sure	

24 Choose the correct prefix to add to these words to change their meaning:

    in-   il-   im-   ir-

(a) responsible	**(d)** legible	**(g)** relevant
(b) patient	**(e)** correct	**(h)** active
(c) moral	**(f)** perfect	

➔ Vocabulary

In this section you will learn to use alliteration. This is a string of words that all start with the same sound and is often found in poems. It draws attention to the words. For example:

the **s**mooth, **s**lippery **s**nake **s**lithered over the **s**and

ten **t**all **t**rees **t**oppled over

The sound at the start of the word needs to be the same, even if it is spelled differently. For example:

he took **f**ive **f**antastic **ph**otos

25 Copy out these sentences and underline the alliteration:

(a) The long, lithe lizard lounged lazily in the sun.

(b) Wild winds whistled through the forest.

(c) Beetles burrowed busily into the old log.

(d) Under the shimmering sea swam the silent, sinister sharks.

(e) The very venomous viper vanished into the grass.

26 Write a sentence containing alliteration about these nouns:

(a) tiger   (c) dog   (e) woman

(b) monkey   (d) cat

Speaking and listening

27 Find and learn some tongue twisters and perform them to your class. For example, 'She sells sea shells on the seashore.'

➡ Writing

In this section you are going to learn to write an explanation text. This is a piece of writing that explains how something works or what it is like. You read an explanation text about beetles earlier in this chapter. An explanation text has the following features:

- It has a title, which shows what the explanation is about.
- It is written in the present tense.
- It uses subheadings to organise the information.
- It may use time words and phrases to put things in order – for example, then, next, finally.

- The vocabulary is specific to the topic.
- There may be diagrams or pictures, with labels, to help the reader to understand what is being explained.

In order to write an explanation text, you first need to understand how the thing you are going to write about works. This means doing some research. You might use the library or the internet, or you might talk to a person who knows a lot about the subject already (an expert).

Imagine you are going to write an explanation about how bees make honey. Here is an example:

Title, which shows what is being explained

Subheadings to divide up the text. The process is divided into short steps to make it clear.

A labelled diagram to help the reader understand what is being explained

How bees make honey

Introduction

We all enjoy the sweet taste of honey on our toast in the morning, but where does it actually come from? We have the bee to thank for this delicious treat and making it is not an easy task. There are many steps before the honey is ready to eat.

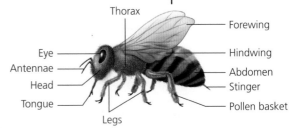

Collecting the pollen

When you see bees buzzing around your garden, they are not just having fun. By travelling from flower to flower, bees collect nectar from the blossoms and store it in a special stomach. They suck out the nectar with their mouths.

To the hive

Next, when they are full of nectar, the bees go back to their hive and pass the nectar onto other bees who chew on it. This is how it turns into thick, sticky honey. The honey is then stored in the honeycomb cells. Finally, the bees have to dry the honey out to make it stickier by flapping their wings. It is a slow process and it can take eight bees a whole lifetime to make just one teaspoonful of honey.

Time words

Present tense

Words that are specific to bees and making honey

A good way to check if your explanation text is successful is to give it to a friend and ask them if they understand what you have written about. If not, make the language simpler and break the text down into more steps to make it clearer.

Try writing explanation texts about these topics. You will need to do some research first, to make sure you understand the subject before you start.

28 Write an explanation of how caterpillars turn into butterflies.

29 Write an explanation of how spiders spin their webs.

30 Write an explanation of how birds build their nests.

31 Write an explanation of how bats navigate in the dark.

Back in time

It's no coincidence that the word 'history' ends in the word 'story'. Some of the best stories in the world were inspired by real events and reading about people who might really have existed can be thrilling. In this chapter you will read stories set in specific periods of history. Is there a period of history that you find interesting and would like to write a story about?

Skill focus: Inference

In this chapter you will have another opportunity to practise inference questions. You will need to find clues in the text to help you answer the questions. You will also begin to copy words from the text into your answer. These help to show how you worked the answer out and are called quotations.

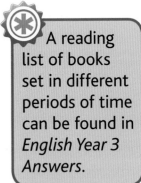

A reading list of books set in different periods of time can be found in *English Year 3 Answers*.

⮕ Comprehension

As you learnt in Chapter 2, some questions don't have obvious answers. You have to find clues in order to answer them. Some questions also ask you to show how you worked out the answer. You can do this by copying one of the clues from the text into your answer. If you need to do this, you might see some of the following words in the question:

- Give evidence from the text.

- Give a reason for your answer.

- Copy something from the text to support your answer.

- Refer to the text/passage in your answer.

- How do you know?
- What evidence is there for your answer?
- Give a quotation to support/back up your answer.

When you copy something directly from the text, you need to show that you have done this by using speech marks around the copied words. This shows that they are not your own words and are a quotation. For example:

I know it was winter because it says, 'the freezing snow fell gently from the sky'.

There are other ways you could phrase your answer:

> I know it was winter because 'the freezing snow fell gently from the sky'.
>
> It was winter. The evidence is: 'the freezing snow fell gently from the sky'.

These words were copied directly from the text so they must have speech marks around them.

It is also important to remember that when you are writing by hand it is usual to use a pair of speech marks each time: " ". Stories that appear in print, however, often use single speech marks: ' '.

Now look at this passage:

> As she stood on the start line, her knees were quivering and her heart was beating loud and fast in her chest. It felt like her trainers were glued to the track. The crowd was roaring all around her but it sounded like it was a thousand miles away, not just a few metres. The finish line was only a blur and Karina could feel the beads of sweat begin to drip down her face.

1 What do you think Karina is about to do? Refer to the text in your answer. (2 marks)

There are a few clues in the text, which are highlighted in green. Use them to work out what Karina might be doing and then use one of the clues as your quotation. Your answer might look like this:

> I think Karina is about to run in a race. (1 mark) I think this because the text says, 'she stood on the start line'. (1 mark)

2 How is Karina feeling? How do you know? (2 marks)

Again, think about the evidence. What is Karina doing or thinking that might give you a clue about how she is feeling? When you have worked it out, choose some words from the passage that back up your idea. You will score 1 mark for naming a feeling and 1 for a quotation from the passage.

> Now try to answer these questions yourself. For question 1, use a different quotation in your answer.

Try this comprehension exercise, using the guidance above to help you answer the questions. Inference questions are in bold.

Moving to the country

> Edie and her family lived in London during the Second World War. In this passage she describes what it was like to be evacuated with her brother Tom while the rest of the family stayed in London. Evacuation was common during the war, as children were sent away from London to live in the countryside, where it was safer.

Our train was supposed to leave Paddington station in West London at eight this morning. Dad's boss – Mr Abbott – was a star and took us there in his Austin.

'You didn't need to do this, Reg,' my dad said as Mr Abbott stood on the doorstep, stifling a yawn.

5 'Course I did, Bert,' said Mr Abbott. 'At least you'll know the nippers have done one bit of the journey safely. Are you fit?'

We hugged Mum and Shirl tearfully and I smoothed Chamberlain's beautiful ears back one last time.

'Be good,' said Mum pointedly to Tom, looking him deep in the eyes. 'Do what Edie
10 tells you. I'll be thinking of you every other minute, I shouldn't wonder.' And before she lost control, she bundled us into the back of the car with a final kiss. Only Shirl stayed on the pavement to wave us goodbye.

'Don't get too used to having the room to yourself,' I shouted at her through the window. 'We're not going to be that long.'

15 She grinned. 'I promise,' she said. 'What am I going to do with no one to moan at?'

Under the curved metal roof of Paddington station where the smoke from the locomotives[1] hung greasily in the girders[2], we said our second lot of goodbyes.

■ Children about to be evacuated at Paddington Station in London, 1940

Tom and I found ourselves seats, and pulled down the window in the compartment, squeezing our heads round the blackout blind.

20 'We're not going to hang around,' Dad shouted. 'Going home to get some shut-eye.' And suddenly we were on our own.

When the little slow train from Cardiff at last pulled into Llantrisant station it was five o'clock and even Tom had had enough of trains for one day. The platform was eerily quiet apart from the hissing of steam and the birds tweeting. Bushes hung over the
25 fences looking badly in need of a haircut. We were the only passengers getting off, but as if there was any danger of missing us, a scowling man stood by the station building holding a piece of cardboard high in the air. On it was scrawled the one word: 'BENSON'. The writing was worse than Tom's. The man was overweight and bald. A pair of leather braces barely kept his stomach and his dirty trousers from falling apart.

30 'That's got to be Mr James,' I said, pulling our battered old suitcase out of the carriage on to the gravelled platform.

'He doesn't look very pleased to see us,' Tom muttered.

From *My Story: The Blitz* by Vince Cross

[1] locomotive = train
[2] girder = metal bar that holds up the roof

3 Who took the family to the station? (1 mark)

4 How did they travel to the station? (1 mark)

5 **Who or what do you think Chamberlain is? How do you know? (2 marks)**

6 **How do you think the children's mother felt about her children leaving? Give a reason from the text for your answer. (2 marks)**

7 **Who do you think Shirl is? Give a reason for your answer. (2 marks)**

8 **Why do you think the children's father didn't stay long at the station? Refer to the text in your answer. (2 marks)**

9 Choose two words of your own to describe the station at Llantrisant. (2 marks)

10 **How did the children know that Mr James wasn't very pleased to see them? (2 marks)**

Speaking and listening

11 Take turns to sit in the 'hot seat' at the front of the classroom and answer questions in the role of Edie or Tom, the characters in the passage above. Questioners could ask you how you feel about being evacuated, what the journey was like or what you think of Mr James.

Now try this comprehension exercise. It is another first person account.

Living in Pompeii

Claudia is a young girl living in Pompeii during Roman times. She has few friends and her mother is rather unkind. She is also worried about the way the ground has been shaking as Pompeii is located near a great volcano: Vesuvius. A year after this passage is set, the volcano erupted, destroying the town.

18 November

I am bored bored bored. It is wet outside, so I cannot even take Pollux out for a walk. Mother says I spend too much time dawdling around the kitchen, and disturbing the slaves at their work. If you're not upsetting them, you are hiding in your room, she
5   says. What do you do in there all the time on your own?

This afternoon some of Mother's friends came to call. I listened to their chatter, wishing I had someone to talk to. I have my diary but it cannot talk to me. I love Pollux dearly, but he cannot talk either. If only I had a friend – a proper friend. Someone I could share secrets with, someone who is not too grown-up to run and
10   jump and play.

20 November

Pollux ran away today. My, I was upset. Mother said it was good riddance. He is a useless guard dog, she said. Samius does not look after him properly, I cried. He is often hungry and thirsty. Is it his fault he runs? He is a greedy dog, Mother said
15   firmly.

I searched for Pollux everywhere. Then I saw that the side gate had swung open. I slipped out. I wouldn't go far, I promised myself. Just along the street.

Outside, the din hit me like a blacksmith's hammer. I despaired. How ever would I find him? How would I hear his bark?

20   At Vastus's new bakery I hesitated. I was about to scuttle past when a big man lurched out of the entrance. 'Mind yourself,' he growled, rudely shoving past me.

But Pollux was nowhere to be seen. Sadly, I wended my way home. I was almost back when I heard a bark. I knew that bark. Quickly I turned round.

A bedraggled Pollux leaped for my lap, trailing his chain behind him. His ear was
25   torn. He whimpered plaintively as I touched it.

'Oh Pollux! How did you hurt your ear?' I cried, cuddling him.

From *My Story: Pompeii* by Sue Reid

12 Why is Claudia bored at the start of the passage? (2 marks)

13 How do you think Claudia feels about her life? Refer to the passage in your answer. (2 marks)

14 Who or what is Pollux? (1 mark)

15 How does Mother feel about Pollux? Give a reason for your answer. (2 marks)

16 How do you know that Claudia really cares for Pollux? Give two examples from the passage. (2 marks)

17 What condition was Pollux in when Claudia found him? Refer to the text in your answer. (2 marks)

18 Write down one thing about Claudia's life in Pompeii that is very different from your own life, and one thing that is similar. (2 marks)

Speaking and listening

19 Working in small groups, act out what happens in *Living in Pompeii*. Read the passage through again and think about how many characters you will need and what everyone does. Don't forget the angry man at the bakery and Claudia's grumpy mother.

→ Grammar

Different stories are written from different points of view. Depending on who is telling the story, we say it is written in the first person or the third person.

First and third person

A story written in the first person is told by one of the characters in the story. A story written in the third person is told from the point of view of a narrator who is not part of the story.

Different words are used in the story depending on whether it is written in the first person or the third person:

First person: I   we   our   my   mine   me   us

Third person: He   she   it   they   them   his   hers   their

For example:

First person: As **I** stepped outside, **I** felt the warm sun on **my** skin.

Third person: As **she** stepped outside, **she** felt the warm sun on **her** skin.

As **John** stepped outside, **he** felt the warm sun on **his** skin.

As **the children** stepped outside, **they** felt the warm sun on **their** skin.

Many stories are written in the third person, but some are written in the first person, such as the two comprehension passages that you have read in this chapter. Diaries are always written in the first person.

---

20 Decide whether each sentence is written in the first or third person:

  (a) We all went to the museum together.

  (b) History is my favourite subject.

  (c) She was interested in learning about the Romans.

  (d) Our favourite school trip was to the Viking museum.

  (e) They acted out the Battle of Hastings in their assembly.

21 Copy out these sentences and underline the words that tell you whether they are written in the first person or the third person:

  (a) She went to the library to renew her book about Henry VIII.

  (b) My family and I took our cameras to the museum to take photos.

  (c) The dog dug up a gold coin when it was burying its bone in the garden.

  (d) The Vikings invaded Britain in their longboats.

  (e) I visited my friend's house and told her my favourite story about the ancient Egyptians.

⬌ Punctuation

We use apostrophes to show when something belongs to something or someone. They look like a comma but up high ('). It is important to know where to put them in a sentence.

Apostrophes for possession

Apostrophes are used to show belonging. If someone or something owns, possesses or has something, you add -'s after the word for the owner. For example:

The man owns a boat. It is the **man's** boat.

The child owns a book. It is the **child's** book.

You don't have to have bought something to possess it. It might be something you just have. For example:

The dog has a tail. It is the **dog's** tail.

Simon has an idea. It is **Simon's** idea.

■ Waqar has a cake. It is Waqar's cake.

---

22 Copy out these sentences and add in the missing apostrophes:

(a) The womans handbag was made of leather.

(b) Christophers bag was very heavy.

(c) The birds beak was sharp.

(d) My coats zip got stuck.

(e) The teachers pen ran out of ink.

(f) The tables surface was wet.

(g) The flowers stem was green.

(h) The mother held her babys hand.

23 Rewrite these sentences so that they include apostrophes: For example:

The boy owns a football   It is the boy's football.

(a) The pupil owns a pencil case.

(b) The house has a chimney.

(c) Sunita owns a computer.

(d) The cat has a toy.

(e) Sarah has a dream.

⮕ Spelling

In English, there are some words that sound the same but have a different meaning and are spelled differently. These are called homophones. It is important to know the difference between them. For example:

see: to look at something   sea: the water you swim in at the beach

here: in this place   hear: to listen to something

It is a good idea to think of some ways to remember which is which. For example:

You **hear** with your **ear**.

24 Match up the words that sound the same:

(a) bare   **(i)**   whether

(b) meat   **(ii)**   heal

(c) heel   **(iii)**   bury

(d) plain   **(iv)**   bear

(e) weather   **(v)**   not

(f) grown   **(vi)**   plane

(g) berry   **(vii)**   meet

(h) knot   **(viii)**   groan

25 Copy out these sentences, correcting the spelling mistakes:

(a) Plains were used in the Second World War.

(b) I don't know weather I'd rather have been an ancient Greek or an ancient Roman.

(c) Ancient Egyptians believed that they should berry the dead with their precious possessions.

(d) There are many people from history that I would like to meat.

(e) Henry VIII was knot a kind king.

(f) In the past, herbs were used to heel the sick.

(g) Queen Victoria took the throne before she was fully groan up.

➲ Vocabulary

When you are writing about the past, you need to use vocabulary that fits with that period of time. Your writing will sound much more authentic if you mention things from that period of history. For example:

You might set your Victorian story in a **workhouse**.

A Roman character will wear a **toga** and **sandals**.

It's always good to write about a time or setting that you already know lots about. If you want to write about a different time in history, do some research first so that your story sounds believable.

26 Here are some items of clothing from different periods of time. Match them to the historical period(s) they are most associated with: Roman, Victorian or Tudor.

| toga | top hat | doublet and hose | petticoats |
| tunic | corset | school cap | |

27 Here are some settings. Work out which period of time they might be associated with. Use a dictionary to help you.

| workhouse | trench | forum | bath house |
| amphitheatre | bomb shelter | steam train | factory |

➜ Writing

In this chapter you have read two extracts from diaries written by people who lived in the past. In this section you will be writing some diary extracts.

A diary is used to write about things that have happened to the writer. In particular, they are used to describe reactions to, and feelings about, events of the day. They are written after something has happened and give the writer a place to write about their hopes, dreams, worries and other feelings.

Diaries are written in the past tense and the first person.
They include:

- descriptions of things that have happened
- varied and relevant vocabulary
- the writer's feelings about what has happened
- ideas about why things happened and/or what might happen next.

A plan for a diary extract should contain:

- an introduction to set the scene
- descriptions of what has happened
- an ending, which shows how you feel and what might happen next.

Imagine you are asked to write a diary about the best day at school ever. It might begin like this:

Start with 'Dear diary'.   Set the scene. What are you going to write about?

Dear diary,

What a day! I like school but I've never liked it as much as I did today. I still can't stop smiling because the day was so exciting and memorable.

When I first arrived, everything seemed normal. I sat down in class, waiting for my teacher, but instead of Mrs Jenkins, in strolled the Prime Minister. Apparently one of my classmates had won a competition to have her come and teach a lesson at his school. I was speechless when she called my name for the register!

Describe what happened.   Write how you felt when things happened.

28 Imagine you have just got home from the most surprising day of your life. Explain what happened and how it made you feel in your diary.

29 Imagine you can travel back in time. Write your diary after a day visiting a different period of history. What happened? Who did you meet? What did you see? What did you learn? How did you feel?

30 Choose a period of history that you know a lot about. Write a diary extract for a typical day in the life of a person living at that time. Make it clear whose diary it is.

31 Write a short description of an exciting day. Write it once in the first person and then again in the third person.

Imaginary worlds

One of the great joys of being a writer is creating people, places and even words. Roald Dahl is well known for inventing words to make his stories come to life. Reading his stories can be challenging for the reader, but the words he makes up help the reader to better imagine the weird and wonderful characters he describes. Could you create your own whimsical and wacky words?

 A reading list of books in which the author has invented new worlds, creatures, settings or language can be found in *English Year 3 Answers*.

➔ Comprehension

Whenever anybody is reading they come across words they don't know, and it's important to try to work out what the words mean so that you can understand the text better.

There are a few things you can do to work out what a word means:

- Does it look like another word you know? Lots of words belong to word families that might look familiar.

- Does it have any letters at the beginning that give you a clue to its meaning? For example, if it begins with un-, you know it's probably the opposite of the rest of the word because un- means 'not'.

- Does it describe something? If it does, ask yourself what you know about that thing already. The describing word might be similar.

Have a look at the passage below:

> Amar had walked for hours. His feet were tired and his legs were **fatigued.** In fact, his whole body was exhausted. The rain was beginning to fall and the temperature was dropping. He was feeling **anxious** because he was worried he wouldn't get home before sunset. He knew he'd be in trouble when he got home. His mother would be cross but his father would be worse. He would be **incensed.** Amar had promised he would only go out for half an hour. He hadn't realised how easily he could get lost.

1 What does the word 'fatigued' mean? (1 mark)

Look at the sentence the word is in. The word 'fatigued' describes Amar's legs. What has he been doing? What else is happening to his body? Think about what might make sense. His feet are tired and his whole body is exhausted. It makes sense that his legs would be tired too. Your answer might look like this:
   The word 'fatigued' means tired. (1 mark)

2 What does the word 'anxious' mean? (1 mark)

Look at the sentence that is highlighted in yellow. It must be a feeling. Think about how Amar is feeling at this point in the story.

3 What does the word 'incensed' mean? (1 mark)

The word describes Amar's father. Think about what else is said nearby about Amar's father (look at the text highlighted in blue).

> Now answer questions 2 and 3 yourself.

Try this comprehension exercise, using the simple steps above to help you answer the questions. Questions about word meaning in context are in bold.

Dinner with the BFG

> Would you like to have dinner with a giant? Although this giant is friendly, Sophie isn't very keen on his giant food.

The BFG was still holding the awesome snozzcumber in his right hand, and now he put one end into his mouth and bit off a huge hunk of it. He started crunching it up and the noise he made was like the crunching of lumps of ice.

'It's **filthing**!' he spluttered, speaking with his mouth full and spraying large pieces of
5 snozzcumber like bullets in Sophie's direction. Sophie hopped around on the table-top,
ducking out of the way.

'It's **disgusterous**!' the BFG gurgled. 'It's **sickable**! It's **rotsome**! It's **maggotwise**! Try
it yourself, this **foulsome** snozzcumber!'

'No, thank you,' Sophie said, backing away.

10 'It's all you're going to be guzzling around here from now on so you might as well get
used to it,' said the BFG. 'Go on, you snipsy little winkle, have a go!'

Sophie took a small nibble. 'Uggggggggh!' she spluttered. 'Oh no! Oh gosh! Oh help!'
She spat it out quickly. 'It tastes of frogskins!' she gasped. 'And rotten fish!'

'Worse than that!' cried the BFG, roaring with laughter. 'To me it is tasting of
15 clockcoaches and slime-wanglers!'

'Do we really have to eat it?' Sophie said.

'You do unless you is wanting to become so thin you will be disappearing into a thick ear.'

'Into thin air,' Sophie said. 'A thick ear is something quite different.'

Once again that sad winsome look came into the BFG's eyes. 'Words,' he said, 'is oh
20 such a **twitch-tickling** problem to me all my life. So you must simply try to be patient
and stop squibbling. As I am telling you before, I know exactly what words I am
wanting to say, but somehow or other they is always getting squiff-squiddled around.'

'That happens to everyone,' Sophie said.

'Not like it happens to me,' the BFG said. 'I is speaking the most terrible wigglish.'

25 'I think you speak beautifully,' Sophie said.

'You do?' cried the BFG, suddenly brightening. 'You really do?'

'Simply beautifully,' Sophie repeated.

'Well, that is the nicest present anybody is ever giving me in my whole life!' cried the
BFG. 'Are you sure you is not twiddling my leg?'

30 'Of course not,' Sophie said. 'I just love the way you talk.'

'How **wondercrump**!' cried the BFG, still beaming. 'How **whoopsey-splunkers**!
How absolutely **squiffling**! I is all of a stutter.'

From *The BFG* by Roald Dahl

---

4 **Look at the words in bold in the passage. Make a list of the words
that mean something good or positive and a list of the words that
mean something bad or negative. (10 marks)**

5 **Look at the passage and write a definition for the following words. As they are nonsense words, you can't look them up in a dictionary and they might need explaining in a short phrase or sentence.**

(a) snozzcumber (line 1)   (e) squiff-squiddled (line 22)

(b) disgusterous (line 7)   (f) wigglish (line 24)

(c) slime-wanglers (line 15)   (g) wondercrump (line 31)

(d) squibbling (line 21)

Speaking and listening

6 **With a partner, act out the scene between the BFG and Sophie. Think about actions, facial expression and voices. Try hard to pronounce the giant's made-up words and include them in your role play.**

Now try this comprehension exercise. It is from a play, based on the same book the previous extract came from. Look out for more made-up words.

Tea with the Queen

This play is based on the story of the BFG and his young friend Sophie. In this part they are visiting Buckingham Palace to have breakfast with the Queen and to ask her to stop the other bad giants from eating innocent children.

[Fanfare. Enter the Queen. She beckons on Sophie, who look impressed as she enters the ballroom.]

[The Queen, Sophie and the BFG start their breakfast.]

BFG: By goggles, Your Majester, this stuff is making snozzcumbers taste like
5   swatchwallop.

Queen: I beg your pardon?

Sophie: He has never eaten anything except snozzcumbers before, Your Majesty. They taste revolting.

Queen: They don't seem to have stunted his growth!

■ The BFG and Sophie have tea with the Queen, from the 2016 film *The BFG*

10 **BFG:** Where is the frobscottle, Majester?

Queen: The *what?*

BFG: Delumptious fizzy frobscottle! Everyone must be drinking it. Then we can all be whizzpopping happily together!

Queen: What *does* he mean? What is whizzpopping?

15 **Sophie:** Excuse me, Your Majesty. *[She goes to the BFG]* BFG, there is no frobscottle here and whizzpopping is strictly forbidden.

BFG: What? No whizzpopping? No glumptious music?

Sophie: Absolutely not.

Queen: If he wants to make music, please don't stop him.

20 **Sophie:** It's not exactly music …

BFG: Listen, I can whizzpop perfectly well *without* frobscottle if I is trying hard enough.

Sophie: No! Don't! Please!

Queen: When I'm up in Scotland, they play the bagpipes outside my window while
25 I'm eating. *[To the BFG]* Do play something.

BFG: I has her Majester's permission!

[After a moment's concentration, a very loud and long whizzpopper rents the air, perhaps causing the lighting to flicker. Everyone reacts.]

Whoopee! How's that, Majester?

30 **Queen:** I think I prefer the bagpipes.

[But she smiles, to Sophie's relief.]

Comprehension

Now, to business. Sophie, you have told me of your visit to Giant Country and of the giants' ghastly night-time children-eating raids. But before we decide what is to be done, I must confirm the facts. Big Friendly Giant, last night your … er … colleagues raided England. Where did they go the night before?

BFG: I think, Your Majester, they was galloping off to Sweden. They is liking the Sweden sour taste.

Queen: Right. Mr Tibbs, the telephone.

From *The BFG: Plays for Children* adapted by David Wood

---

7 Where does this scene take place? (1 mark)

8 What do you think the BFG means when he says 'By goggles' (line 4)? (1 mark)

9 What does the Queen mean when she says 'They don't seem to have stunted his growth!' (line 9)? (2 marks)

10 Write a definition for the following words, as used in the passage:

    (a) swatchwallop (line 5)   (1 mark)

    (b) frobscottle (line 10)   (1 mark)

    (c) delumptious (line 12)   (1 mark)

    (d) whizzpopping (line 13)   (1 mark)

11 Find two other made-up words the BFG uses when speaking and copy them down. (2 marks)

12 Why do you think the author has made the BFG speak in such an unusual way? Give two ideas. (2 marks)

Speaking and listening

13 Can you imagine feasting on snozzcumbers or drinking frobscottle? How would you feel? Close your eyes and imagine it. Then describe this feeling, using as many interesting adjectives as you can. Don't forget that one of these is delicious and one is disgusting.

→ Grammar

There are different types of sentence that you might read or write.

Types of sentences

Sentences are made up of clauses. A clause is a part of a sentence with a verb in it. Some sentences only have one clause. For example:

The BFG ate a snozzcumber.

Sophie drank the frobscottle.

These are called simple sentences or single-clause sentences.

You can join two clauses together using a conjunction (a joining word). The following words are all conjunctions:

and   or   but   because   when   after   while   so   if   although

For example:

The BFG is kind **because** he doesn't eat children.

Sophie felt sick **when** she ate the snozzcumber.

These are called multi-clause sentences.

Try to use a mixture of sentence types when you write as it makes your writing more interesting to read.

---

14 Decide whether these sentences are single-clauses sentences or multi-clause sentences. Copy out the multi-clause sentences and underline the conjunction.

(a) Roald Dahl made up lots of words.

(b) The BFG speaks weirdly because he is a giant.

(c) Sophie is not afraid of the BFG although he is a giant.

(d) The BFG whizzpopped in front of the Queen.

(e) The Queen smiled when she heard the BFG whizzpopping.

15 Copy and complete these sentences, adding conjunctions from the list above:

(a) Giants live in Giant Country _____ eat children for supper.

(b) The other giants don't like the BFG _____ he is different.

(c) The BFG lives in Giant Country _____ Sophie lives in London.

(d) The BFG hates snozzcumbers _____ he has nothing else to eat.

(e) Sophie likes how the BFG talked _____ she told him.

➔ Punctuation

Later in this chapter, you are going to write a script. Punctuation has to be used carefully in a script, where it is used differently from in a story.

Punctuation for scripts

There are a few important things to remember when you are punctuating a script:

- Don't use speech marks when somebody is talking. In a script, the character names down the left-hand side show who is talking. You don't need speech marks.

- Punctuate what the actors say as you usually would. The actors need the punctuation to help them understand their lines.

- Put any stage directions for the actors in brackets. This shows that the words are not spoken aloud.

For example:

Stage directions are in brackets.

[Curtain up. The BFG is standing by his table, looking down at Sophie, who stands on the table.]

Sophie: BFG, tell me – if you don't eat humans, what do you eat?

BFG: [Sitting] That, little Sophie is a squelching tricky problem. In this sloshflunking Giant Country, happy eats like pineapples and pigwinkles is simply not growing. Nothing is growing except for one extremely icky-poo vegetable. It is called the snozzcumber.

From *The BFG: Plays for Children* adapted by David Wood

Character names are followed by a colon to show who is speaking.

Words spoken are fully punctuated but there are no speech marks.

16 Copy out the play below, correcting the mistakes:

Curtain up.

The BFG's cave is on one side. On the other side, as though in the open air, the Giants are sprawled asleep.

Sophie: 'BFG?'

BFG: Stopping. 'Yes'

Sophie: 'where are you going'

BFG: 'i is going to work'

Sophie: 'Back where i live. blowing your trumpet thing'

BFG: Shocked. 'you is seeing me blowing'

Sophie: 'yes. what were you doing.'

BFG: 'Is i trusting you'

Sophie: 'Of course.'

BFG: 'Well, then I, sophie, is a dream-blowing giant. i blows dreams into the bedrooms of sleeping chiddlers. nice dreams. lovely golden dreams. dreams that is giving the dreamers a happy time.'

From *The BFG: Plays for Children* adapted by David Wood

⬦ Spelling

You have already learnt about some prefixes (letters that go before a word to change its meaning). Here are some more prefixes and their meanings:

■ A subway goes underneath a road.

re- means again or back. For example: revisit means to visit again.

anti- means against. For example: anti-clockwise means against the direction of the clock.

sub- means under. For example: a submarine is a boat that goes under the sea.

auto- means self. For example: automatic means working by itself.

17 Use a dictionary to find the meanings of the following words:

- **(a)** subheading
- **(b)** submerge
- **(c)** antisocial
- **(d)** antiseptic
- **(e)** autobiography
- **(f)** autograph
- **(g)** reappear
- **(h)** redecorate

18 Now use each word in a sentence.

➜ Vocabulary

In this chapter you have come across unusual characters, words and events. Here are some words that describe mysterious, different and unusual things:

offbeat   distinctive   bizarre   peculiar
anomalous   enigmatic   unfathomable ambiguous

19 Use a dictionary to help you write a definition for each word.

20 Write a short story, a poem or a description that uses as many of the words as possible.

➜ Writing

In this chapter you have read an extract from a play and answered questions about it. Now you are going to write your own play.

A script is written to be performed and it has various features designed to make it easy to read and to help the actors to perform it exactly as the writer had planned. These include:

- stage directions telling the actors how to say things and how to move
- character names on the left to show who speaks when
- no speech marks.

At the very start of a script you might also include a cast list and a list of props and costumes.

If your play is longer, you might split it into different scenes, which are set in different locations.

When you are planning what to write your play about, remember that there will be quite a lot of talking. You don't want the actors to be silent for long periods of time, so choose a topic that means there are things to talk about.

Try these activities. Refer to the scripts in this chapter if you are unsure about anything.

21 Write a short play about two people eating a truly disgusting meal. Use appropriate vocabulary and remember to include facial expressions and actions in your stage directions.

22 Write a short play in which two very different people meet for the first time.

23 Write a short play using some made-up words of your own. Think first about why your characters might use made-up words. Do they speak a different language? Are they magical or mystical characters? Are there no real words for what they want to say?

24 Write another scene with Sophie and the BFG as the two main characters. Think about what else they might do together. You don't need to have read the book – just use your imagination.

Risky rescues

A rescue needs a hero and heroics make great stories! No matter what or who is being rescued, these types of stories really do keep the reader on the edge of their seat. Sometimes they are true stories, like in newspapers, but rescues make great fiction too. Can you imagine a risky rescue that you would like to write about?

Skill focus: Fact and opinion

In this chapter you will learn to spot the difference between facts and opinions. Both are important in writing but they are used for different purposes.

A reading list of books about animal rescues and animal rescuers can be found in *English Year 3 Answers*.

→ Comprehension

A fact is something that is known to be true. It may include a number, a percentage, a name or another piece of information that can be proven. A study, a survey, an experiment or some other research may have been carried out to check that it is true. You might have carried out experiments in science to check whether something is true. You will also have come across facts on the news and in newspapers.

An opinion is what somebody thinks about a subject or event. It is not provable. It may be based on facts but somebody else may have a different opinion based on the same facts.

Take a look at this example:

Facts: these details are specific and are easy to prove.

On Wednesday 18th July, officers from the Dog's Family Charity rescued three Border Collies who were found wandering along the edge of the M20 motorway in Kent. The dogs were underfed, thin and dehydrated. They had no collars on and were not micro chipped so it was impossible to find their owners. Nicky Gill, the lead investigator on the rescue, said, 'Sadly, this type of thing is quite common. We believe that the owner has abandoned the dogs because they could not afford to look after them.' The dogs will be taken to the charity's rescue centre and hopefully a new owner will be found.

Opinions: these details are one person's version of what happened. Other people might explain things differently.

1 Find and copy two facts from the text. (2 marks)

Look for things that can be proved true or false. Numbers and names are good things to look for. Your answer might look like this:

Two facts from the text are that the rescue happened on the 18th July (1 mark) and that three Border Collies were rescued (1 mark).

2 What is Nicky Gills' opinion about this event? (2 marks)

Think about what she said about the rescue. Her opinion might not be accurate but you should find it and put it in your answer.

Now try to answer the questions yourself, using different facts to answer question 1.

Try the comprehension exercise on the next page, using the information and examples above to help you answer the questions. Questions about facts and opinions are in bold.

Animal rescues

Here are some real-life rescue stories from the RSPCA (Royal Society for the Prevention of Cruelty to Animals).

Hog-gate

We and the fire service came to the aid of a hedgehog who had gorged on a few too many worms and got himself stuck in a gate in Suffolk over the summer.

The hog misjudged his own girth and got himself stuck between the railings of a
5   gate, in Newmarket, on June 14.

A passer-by spotted the prickly porker in a tight spot and called us. We then turned to local firefighters for help to free him. Specialist equipment was used to widen the bars so he could be lifted out safely.

After spending a night in our care to ensure he was unhurt, the hedgehog was
10   returned to the wild the following day.

Abseiling to safety

Our Inspectors will go to any lengths to save an animal in danger. Andy Broadbent and Mike Pugh proved that in August when they abseiled down a sea cliff to rescue a stranded ewe at Trwyn Cilan near Hell's Mouth Bay, in Abersoch, Wales.

15   It's believed she'd been stuck 20–30 metres down for around two weeks before being caught and hoisted back to safety.

Ferret in a fix

This little ferret found himself in difficulty when he got his body stuck in a metal railing not just once, but twice!

20   The critter, later named Whoops, got his body trapped in fencing in Ossett, West Yorkshire, on November 10.

RSPCA Inspector Charly Wain and firefighters attended to help the little ferret but it was clear they wouldn't be
25   able to free him. So they cut the fence and took him to the vets to be carefully removed.

The ferret, thought to be a stray, was lucky to escape the tricky situation
30   without being hurt and was taken in to be rehomed.

From www.rspca.org.uk

■ A young ferret

3 List the three animals that were rescued in the passage. (1 mark)

4 **Find and copy a fact from the first rescue story, Hog-gate. (1 mark)**

5 'a hedgehog who had gorged on a few too many worms' (lines 2–3). Is this a fact or an opinion? Give a reason for your answer. (2 marks)

6 **What was the opinion, in the second rescue story, about how long the ewe had been on the cliff? (1 mark)**

7 Why do you think the ferret in the third rescue story was named Whoops? (1 mark)

8 **Find and copy an opinion from the third rescue story. (1 mark)**

9 Give a definition for the following words, as used in the passage:

   (a) misjudged (line 4)   (1 mark)

   (b) hoisted (line 16)   (1 mark)

   (c) rehomed (line 31)   (1 mark)

Speaking and listening

10 Hold a discussion about your favourite animals. Give reasons to explain why you like these animals. Is there a most popular animal in the class?

Now try this comprehension exercise. It is also about a rescued animal and contains both facts and opinions.

New Littlest Hobo: Stray German Shepherd travels to over 30 cities after being rescued

This is the story about the international traveller, Spookie the German Shepherd.

MEET the globe-trotting German Shepherd who has probably seen more of the world than you – after travelling to over 30 cities and 12 countries.

Adorable Spookie, from Noe Valley in San Francisco, USA, has been travelling around the US and Europe with her owners Karina and Travis Higgs. Mrs Higgs,
5 28, adopted Spookie at eight-weeks-old after the puppy was found abandoned and walking the streets alone by a pet rescue team. Since then, they have been inseparable and travel together everywhere, especially over the last year where they've visited a remarkable 30 cities and 12 countries.

Spookie's owners joke that the five-year-old gallivanting German Shepherd who loves
10 selfies has a 'true rags to riches' story and that she's seen more of the world than most humans. Mrs Higgs said: 'She's definitely been able to live a life any other dog wouldn't normally have. Some of our friends have commented that Spookie travels more than them and she's seen more than they will in their lifetimes. I would say she's visited over 30 cities and 12 countries this year alone, we've done a lot of travelling. She's quite the
15 explorer and is really funny while travelling as she's always examining things.'

Mrs Higgs adopted her canine companion five years ago, after Spookie was found wandering the streets alone. She added: 'I was walking home when I saw a bunch of adoptable puppies on the corner of the street, I was drawn straight away to this cute all-black German Shepherd. I looked at Spookie and while holding her she gave me a
20 kiss. From there we've always had an amazing bond.'

Mrs Higgs named her pooch Spookie after her unusual fear of everything. Amusingly, now the puppy has grown into a carefree canine who fearlessly travels the world. Her owners say they will continue their adventures with more planned for Spookie next year and believe she can sense when they're set to travel again. Mrs Higgs said:
25 'As soon as the suitcases come out, she knows she's going travelling and gets very excitable.' Next year Spookie will extend her list of place she's seen after visiting London, Paris, Rome, Portugal, Finland and more.

Slightly adapted from www.express.co.uk

11 What is the name of the dog that is rescued in the story? (1 mark)

12 Decide whether these quotations are facts or opinions:

(a) 'Meet the globe-trotting German Shepherd who has probably seen more of the world than you' (1 mark)

(b) 'Spookie, from Noe Valley in San Francisco, USA' (1 mark)

(c) 'Mrs Higgs adopted her canine companion five years ago' (1 mark)

(d) 'Her owners [...] believe she can sense when they're set to travel again.' (1 mark)

(e) 'Mrs Higgs, 28, adopted Spookie at eight-weeks-old' (1 mark)

13 What does the writer mean by 'rags to riches' (line 10)? (2 marks)

14 'I would say she's visited over 30 cities and 12 countries this year alone.' Is this a fact or an opinion? Give a reason for your answer. (2 marks)

15 Do you think Spookie is a suitable name for this dog? Give a reason for your answer. (2 marks)

Speaking and listening

16 Act out a rescue scene that you have read about with a group of friends. Think about the different characters, their feelings and actions. Try to make it dramatic.

→ Grammar

When you are writing, it's important to have an understanding of the different verb tenses: past, present and future. In this section you will focus on the past tense.

Verb tenses

All verbs can be used in the past, present and future tenses. There are two types of past tense that you can use.

The simple past tense

The simple past tense is usually formed by adding -ed to the verb. For example:

Present tense		Simple past tense	
I talk	We talk	I talked	We talked
You talk		You talked	
He/she/it talks	They talk	He/she/it talked	They talked

For some verbs, the simple past tense looks quite different from the present tense. We call these verbs irregular verbs. 'Think' is an irregular verb:

Present tense		Simple past tense	
I think	We think	I thought	We thought
You think		You thought	
He/she/it thinks	They think	He/she/it thought	They thought

Some other irregular verbs and their simple past tense include:

run ⟶ ran   begin ⟶ began   come ⟶ came   fall ⟶ fell

eat ⟶ ate   find ⟶ found   give ⟶ gave   go ⟶ went

have ⟶ had   hear ⟶ heard   make ⟶ made   say ⟶ said

see ⟶ saw   sit ⟶ sat   take ⟶ took   write ⟶ wrote

The present perfect tense

There is another version of the past tense called the present perfect tense. It shows that an event has passed and finished. You can use it to show in what order things happened in the past.

For the present perfect tense, you use the verb 'have' before the simple past of the main verb. For example:

Present tense		Present perfect tense	
I talk	We talk	I **have** talked	We **have** talked
You talk		You **have** talked	
He/she/it talks	They talk	He/she/it **has** talked	They **have** talked

17 Copy out these sentences, correcting the mistakes:

(a) He runned to stop the horse from bolting through the gate.

(b) We heared about the rescue on the radio.

(c) The cat almost falled into the pond.

(d) Everybody sawed the rescue reported on the TV.

(e) The man taked a big risk to save the cat from the tree.

18 Change these sentences from the simple past tense to present perfect tense:

(a) The man rescued the dog from the river.

(b) We locked the car door.

(c) I helped the man pick up his shopping.

(d) They wrote about the rescue in the newspaper.

(e) You saw the cat climb up the tree.

→ Punctuation

In a newspaper, reporters often refer to what witnesses and experts said about what happened. When they include words from interviews, they have to use speech marks to show that somebody else said the words.

Direct speech

You should use speech marks to show that someone's words are being directly copied.

- Put the speech marks around the words that the person said, as you would in a story.
- Use a capital letter for the first word somebody says.
- Use normal sentence punctuation inside the speech marks.
- Separate the speaking from the rest of the sentence with punctuation: a comma, a question mark or an exclamation mark.

For example:

Speech marks around
the spoken words

Punctuation inside
the speech marks

'Come quickly!' shouted the man.

The witness said, 'It all happened very quickly.'

Capital letter when somebody
starts speaking

Comma to separate the spoken
words from the rest of the sentence

Remember, the punctuation at the end of the speaking always goes *before* the speech mark.

---

19 Copy out these sentences and add in the missing speech marks:

   (a) How can I help you? asked the policeman.

   (b) Tell me what happened, asked the reporter.

   (c) Help! shouted the young man.

   (d) The boy asked, How did that happen?

   (e) The fireman said, You're safe now.

20 Copy out these sentences and add in all of the missing punctuation:

   (a) what did you see asked the newspaper reporter

   (b) i am so grateful to the rescuer said the cat's owner

   (c) my cat is stuck up the tree cried the man

   (d) the girl shouted I'm over here

   (e) the policeman asked when did you last see your dog

➜ Spelling

You can add suffixes (letters which go after a word) to a verb to change its meaning. For example:

   The suffix -ing can be used for the present tense. For example:
   walk ⟶ walking.

   The suffix -ed is used for the past tense. For example: walk ⟶ walked.

   The suffix -er is used to turn a verb into a noun (a name of a person, place or thing). For example: walk ⟶ walker.

There are some simple rules to remember when adding these suffixes:

1 If the verb ends in an -e, take away the -e before you add the suffix. For example: hike ⟶ hiking ⟶ hiked ⟶ hiker

2 If the verb ends in a -y with a consonant before it, change the -y to an -i, then add the suffix. This is not needed when you add -ing. For example:
   copy ⟶ copied ⟶ copier *but* copying

3 If the verb ends in -y with a vowel before it, just add the suffix. For example:
play ⟶ playing ⟶ played ⟶ player

4 If the verb ends in a consonant, with a single vowel before it, double the consonant before adding the suffix. Never double an '-x'. For example:
drop ⟶ dropping ⟶ dropped ⟶ dropper

5 If the verb ends in a consonant, with a single vowel before it, but the last syllable isn't emphasised, don't double the consonant. For example:
garden ⟶ gardening ⟶ gardened ⟶ gardener

Some verbs are irregular and don't follow this pattern. You will have to learn how to spell words made from irregular verbs separately.

---

21 Copy and complete this table:

	-ing	-ed	-er
clip			
work			
call			
paint			
spray			
carry			
bake			
dance			

22 Copy out this passage, correcting the spelling mistakes. There are 12 words to correct.

Last Thursday afternoon a brave man rescueed a cat that thinked it was a fish and tryed to go swiming. The poor kitty almost drownd as he was not a natural swimer. The young man sawed the cat in the water and finded himself jumping into the river. He grabed the cat, puled it to the riverbank and savd its life. A lucky kitty indeed.

➔ Vocabulary

When you are using speech in your writing, it is easy to overuse the word 'said'. There are many words that you can use instead of 'said'. Words with similar meanings are called synonyms and each synonym means something slightly different. Take a look at the list below:

Said normally: announced, declared, stated, remarked

Said in response to a question: responded, replied

Said as a question: requested, enquired

Said loudly: shouted, exclaimed, yelled, bellowed

Said quietly: murmured, whispered, mumbled

Said angrily: fumed, thundered, snapped, grumbled

Said sadly: sobbed, whimpered, cried

Said in fear: stammered, stuttered

---

23 Copy out these sentences, replacing the word 'said' with a better alternative. Use the list above to help you.

(a) 'What a horrible dream!' said James.

(b) Samir said, 'Hurry up!'

(c) The teacher said, 'Did you hear that sound?'

(d) The child said, 'I've lost my teddy.'

(e) The inspector said, 'What has happened?'

➔ Writing

In this section, you are going to write a newspaper report. The purpose of a newspaper report is to inform people about events that have recently happened. It should contain facts about an event and the opinions of witnesses to the event but not the writer's own opinion.

A newspaper report has a particular structure:

- It begins with a headline – a catchy title for the report.
- The opening paragraph summarises the entire story in two or three sentences.
- The middle paragraphs contain more details about the story, told in time order (chronologically). Interviews with witnesses or victims might be included. Experts might also be interviewed.
- The closing paragraph is a summary of what has happened and what is expected to happen next.

Also remember that newspaper reports:

- are written in the third person and in the past tense
- are written in formal (grown-up) language
- contain facts
- should answer the five Ws: Who? When? What? Where? Why?

Imagine you are writing a newspaper report about the hedgehog that was rescued in the first comprehension passage. It might start like this:

Catchy headline   Facts   Past tense and third person   Opening paragraph to summarise the whole story

Wedge-hog

A tubby hedgehog had a lucky escape this week when he became wedged in between two gate posts. The RSPCA were on hand to free him.

On Saturday 23rd July, Joe Cox and his friend Russ Stapleton were going for their usual afternoon bike ride. They had set off at 4 p.m. As they approached the boundary of Tidemouth Farm, they hoisted their bikes over the gate to cross to the next footpath. Suddenly they heard a squeaking and scratching sound under their feet.

When they saw the hedgehog, they thought it was just chattering, but they soon realised it was in trouble. Mr Cox remembered, 'We saw that the hedgehog had wedged itself between the bars of the gate. Perhaps he had eaten too many worms!'

Quoted words from a witness   Opinions

Now have a go at these newspaper writing tasks.

24 Choose another one of the rescue stories that you have read in this chapter, and turn it into a newspaper report. You can invent witnesses to interview and add any more information you need.

25 Choose a familiar nursery rhyme or fairy tale and write a newspaper article about it. Perhaps the story of how Bo Peep lost her sheep, or the tragic tale of the three little pigs whose houses were almost all blown down?

26 Write a newspaper article about something that has happened in your local area, town or school recently. Do some research on the internet or in local papers to find the facts.

27 Write an article about an imaginary rescue, where a superhero saves the day. You can invent the superhero and give them special powers that help them during the rescue.

Wild animals

Many adventures have taken place in lands full of wild and rare animals. The thrill of danger, the wonder of seeing new and beautiful creatures and the sheer excitement of being near nature has inspired many writers. By reading these stories, you will learn about these amazing animals and, hopefully, be motivated to find out more about them and write about them yourself. Which animals are you most curious about?

Skill focus: Joining the dots

In this chapter, you will have a chance to practise all of the skills you have learnt in the previous four chapters. This includes: summary, drawing inferences and using quotations, working out the meaning of unknown words, and identifying facts and opinions.

A reading list of books about Africa can be found in *English Year 3 Answers*.

→ Comprehension

Here are some reminders of how to tackle the different types of questions you will come across in the next two comprehension exercises:

- When you are asked to **summarise**:
  - Think about the whole paragraph, verse or piece of text.
  - Pick out the most important parts.
  - Think of words that you could use to describe the piece.
- When you answer **inference questions**:
  - Look for clues to help you work out the answer.
  - The answer won't be immediately obvious, so you will have to think about it.

- If you need to use some words or phrases from the passage in your answer, put speech marks around them to show that they are not your own words.

- Look for clues in the question and the number of marks to see if you need to use quotations from the passage.

- When you are trying to work out **what a word means**:
  - Find the word in the passage and read that part again.
  - Use the meaning of the rest of the sentence or paragraph to help you.
  - Think about whether the word is a verb, a noun or an adjective.
  - Put your idea in place of the original word and check it makes sense.

- When you are looking for **facts and opinions**:
  - Think about whether the information is certain or true. If it is, it is likely to be a fact.
  - Facts may include numbers, names, dates and other provable pieces of information.
  - Opinions are what somebody thinks. They may be different for different people.

Now try this comprehension exercise, using what you have already learnt to help you. There are a range of questions, and you will need to use all of the skills you have been practising to answer them.

Worth the wait

> Living in Africa, Bertie has developed a great interest in wild animals, and the waterhole he can see from his house proves to be full of surprises ...

There was a waterhole downhill from the farmhouse, and some distance away. That waterhole, when there was water in it, became Bertie's whole world. He would spend hours in the dusty compound, his hands gripping the fence, looking out at the wonders of the veld[1], at the giraffes drinking, spread-legged, at the waterhole; at the
5 browsing impala, tails twitching, alert; at the warthogs snorting and snuffling under the shade of the shingayi trees; at the baboons, the zebras, the wildebeests, and the elephants bathing in the mud. But the moment Bertie always longed for was when a

pride of lions came padding out of the veld. The impala were the first to spring away, then the zebra would panic and gallop off. Within seconds the lions would have the 10 waterhole to themselves, and they would crouch to drink.

From the safe haven of the compound Bertie looked and learned as he grew up. By now, he could climb the tree by the farmhouse, and sit high in its branches. He could see better from up there. He would wait for his lions for hours on end. He got to know the life of the waterhole so well that he could feel the lions were out there, even 15 before he saw them.

Bertie had no friends to play with, but he always said he was never lonely as a child. At night he loved reading his books and losing himself in the stories, and by day his heart was out in the veld with the animals. That was where he yearned to be. Whenever his mother was well enough, he would beg her to take him outside the 20 compound, but her answer was always the same.

'I can't, Bertie. Your father has forbidden it,' she'd say. And that was that …

… Week in, week out, Bertie had to stay behind his fence. He made up his mind though, that if no-one would take him out into the veld, then one day he would go by himself. But something always held him back. Perhaps it was one of those tales 25 he'd been told of black mamba snakes whose bite would kill you within ten minutes, of hyenas whose jaws would crunch you to bits, of vultures who would finish off anything that was left so that no-one would ever find even the bits. For the time being he stayed behind the fence. But the more he grew up, the more his compound became a prison to him.

30 One evening – Bertie must have been about six years old by now – he was sitting high up in the branches of his tree, hoping against hope the lions might come down for their sunset drink as they often did. He was thinking of giving up, for it would soon be too dark to see much now, when he saw a solitary lioness come down to the waterhole. Then he saw that she was not alone. Behind her, and on unsteady legs, 35 came what looked like a lion cub – but it was white, glowing white in the gathering gloom of dusk.

While the lioness drank, the cub played at catching her tail; and then, when she had had her fill, the two of them slipped away into the long grass and were gone.

From *The Butterfly Lion* by Michael Morpurgo

> [1]veld = open country or grassland in Africa

111

1 Which animals did Bertie often see under the shade of the shingayi tree? (1 mark)

2 Where did Bertie go to get a better view of the animals? (1 mark)

3 Summarise in your own words why Bertie didn't go out into the veld by himself. (2 marks)

4 Why do you think this passage is called 'Worth the wait'? (2 marks)

5 Choose an adjective of your own to describe Bertie. Give a reason for your answer. (2 marks)

6 Do you think Bertie was happy? Refer to the passage in your answer. (2 marks)

7 Give another word for the following, as used in the passage:

(a) crouch (line 10)   (1 mark)

(b) haven (line 11)   (1 mark)

(c) yearned (line 18)   (1 mark)

(d) solitary (line 33)   (1 mark)

Speaking and listening

8 Look again at 'Worth the wait'. Working with a partner, prepare a short role play in which one of you is Bertie and the other is his mother. Bertie has just returned from his lookout post where he saw a lion cub. He's very excited!

Try the following comprehension exercise. It is a newspaper report. Think back to when you wrote newspaper reports to help you understand the purpose of the text and the type of language used.

Elephant family

The newspaper article is about a new arrival at Chester Zoo.

Rare baby elephant born in Chester Zoo

A rare Asian elephant has been born at Chester Zoo.

The unnamed female calf was born
to 12-year-old mother Sundara
5 overnight. Keepers at the zoo said
both mother and daughter are doing
well and visitors will be able to see the
new arrival from Saturday.

The calf is the 19th elephant to be
10 born at Chester Zoo in its 85-year
history and brings the current size of
its herd to seven. Five, including the
new calf, are part of the same family
called the Hi Ways. Elephants are born into captivity in the UK only once or twice a
15 year. Keepers at the zoo watched the birth remotely via CCTV cameras so as not to
disturb the herd. The calf's name will be decided in the coming days.

Richard Fraser, assistant team manager of elephants at Chester Zoo, said: 'The arrival
of a calf is a great family occasion for the elephant herd and brings the whole group
together. She delivered her calf on to soft sand with all the family gathered around.
20 Sundara then gave her a series of little kicks to gently stimulate and encourage her
to her feet. Minutes later, the new arrival was up and standing. There's always a lot of
excitement among the elephants whenever there's a birth. It's a hugely positive event
for the herd.'

Asian elephants are native to South and South East Asia and are listed as endangered.
25 There are between 35,000 and 40,000 in the wild and managed breeding programmes.
They live to approximately 50 to 60 years old. Mike Jordan, collections director at
Chester Zoo, said: 'Sundara's new calf is a fantastic addition to the zoo's Hi Way family
of elephants and we hope that news of her arrival will generate more much-needed
awareness of these incredible animals and the pressures for survival that they are faced
30 with in the wild. In India, Asian elephants are regularly injured and killed in conflicts
with humans. They wander into villages, destroying crops and property as they go,
and this often results in violent reactions by villagers. Chester Zoo's conservation work
in Assam in northern India is, however, successfully helping to reduce these problems,
finding good ways for people and wild elephants to live side by side.'

Adapted from www.telegraph.co.uk

9 What is the name of the newborn elephant calf? (1 mark)

10 Look again at the first and second paragraphs. Find and copy two facts. (2 marks)

11 Why do you think the birth of this baby elephant is so important? Give some evidence from the text in your answer. (2 marks)

12 Why are elephants sometimes not welcome in Indian villages? (2 marks)

13 Give a definition for the following words, as used in the passage:

    (a) captivity (line 14)   (1 mark)

    (b) endangered (line 24)   (1 mark)

    (c) awareness (line 29)   (1 mark)

    (d) conflicts (line 30)   (1 mark)

Speaking and listening

14 Should wild animals be kept in zoos and safari parks? Or should they be left in the wild? Can you think of reasons why we should have zoos? Can you think of reasons why we should not have zoos? Join in a class discussion about whether animals should be kept in zoos and safari parks.

→ Grammar

In this section you will practise the topics you have learnt about already in the previous four chapters. These include headings and subheadings, first and third person, types of sentences and verb tenses.

15 Copy out this passage, changing it from the third person into the first person:

In August, Ben visited a safari park. He was very excited and put his camera in his rucksack to take lots of photos. The first animal he saw was an elephant. It was so much bigger than him! Then he saw lions, tigers, zebras and lots of monkeys. The monkeys were his favourite. They sounded like they were talking to him! He wished he could swing from the trees like that!

16 Copy these sentences, changing them from the present tense into the simple past tense:

(a) I am not afraid of snakes.

(b) We are going to the safari park to see the lions.

(c) The zebras chase each other around the park.

(d) The giraffes eat leaves and grass.

(e) There are 30 or more monkeys at the zoo.

17 Copy these sentences, changing them from the simple past tense into the present perfect tense:

(a) I saw many animals on safari.

(b) Julia went to South Africa on holiday and photographed many animals.

(c) A baby tiger was born at the zoo.

(d) The male lion caught his prey.

(e) The monkeys swung in the trees.

18 Copy and complete these sentences, adding in appropriate conjunctions:

(a) Elephants are endangered _____ people hunt them for their tusks.

(b) Some snakes are poisonous _____ others are not.

(c) Wild animals will often run away _____ you get too close to them.

(d) At the safari park you might see lions _____ you might hear them roaring.

(e) It is important to look after wild animals _____ they do not become extinct.

19 Do some research about an animal that interests you. Write about the animal using the subheadings below:

- Appearance
- Habitat
- Food
- Behaviour

➔ Punctuation

Here you will revise question marks, apostrophes for possession and speech marks.

20 Copy out these sentences, adding either a question mark or a full stop:

(a) Would you like to go on safari

(b) Lions are known as the kings of the jungle

(c) Why are giraffes so tall

(d) How do animal charities prevent elephants from becoming endangered

(e) I wondered how many animals I would see at the zoo

21 Copy out this passage, adding in the missing apostrophes:

As we drove through the safari park, the drivers voice explained what we would see. Suddenly we heard a lions roar in the distance. Then right in front of us, a giraffes head popped out above the trees. We couldnt believe it! Next we felt the ground shaking a little. It was an elephants heavy footsteps. The elephants family was following her. As I looked out of the car window, a monkeys face appeared, grinning right at me.

22 Copy out this passage and add in the missing speech marks:

I've got some good news, said Mum. We're going on holiday.

That's brilliant! shouted Bobby and Max in unison. Where are we going?

We're going to Kenya, replied Dad.

Kenya? Where's that? questioned the boys. Is it in Africa?

It is, boys. We're going to see the wild animals on safari.

⮞ Spelling

Now it is time to practise the spelling rules you have learnt.

23 Add un-, mis- or dis- to these words to make a new word:

(a) afraid

(e) pleasant

(i) usual

(b) natural

(f) connect

(j) cover

(c) behave

(g) treat

(d) agree

(h) honest

24 Each of these words has a prefix. Write a sentence using each word. Try to write about Africa, animals and conservation.

(a) review

(c) submit

(e) recall

(b) antidote

(d) autobiography

(g) subject

25 Copy out this passage, correcting the spelling mistakes. There are 11 to correct.

When we arrivved in Kenya the sun was shinning brightly in the sky. I was so excitted. I was hopping to see some wild animals like elephants and lions. We boarded the bus and the drivver told us that it would take two hours to get to our hotel. I spent the whole journey lookking out of the window. By the time we gotted to our hotel, I had seen monkeys playying in the trees, elephants eatting grass and a lion chassing a deer. I was amazzed.

26 Write sentences using these pairs of homophones. Try to use both in the same sentence if you can.

(a) see / sea

(b) main / mane

(c) plain / plane

(d) scene / seen

(e) weather / whether

➔ Vocabulary

In this section you will have an opportunity to find some new words, using a thesaurus. A thesaurus is a book full of synonyms. Synonyms are words with the same or similar meanings.

To use a thesaurus, you first have to decide on the word that you would like to find other words for. For example, you might decide you want to find other words for 'big'.

The thesaurus is organised alphabetically, like a dictionary. Find your original word in the thesaurus. Next to it you will find a list of similar words.

Beware: the words listed will be similar in meaning to the word you looked up, but not all of them will be right for your writing. Some of these words are 'bigger' than others. A large cake is smaller than a massive cake.

big	**ADJECTIVE** This word is often overused. Here are some alternatives:
1	*a big house* *The bill was very big.*
▶	large, great, huge, enormous, colossal, immense
2	*a big difference*
▶	significant, important, substantial, considerable, sizeable
3	*big ideas*
▶	ambitious, grand, grandiose, far-reaching
4	*That was big of you.*
▶	generous, considerate, magnanimous, kind, gracious

From *Oxford School Thesaurus* edited by Robert Allen

27 Use a thesaurus to find synonyms for the following words:

(a) happy

(b) sad

(c) walk

(d) run

(e) say

(f) good

(g) bad

(h) see

28 Now try to group or order each set of synonyms in different ways. For example, you could order the synonyms for 'happy' from happiest to least happy, or the synonyms for 'walk' from fastest walk to slowest walk.

⟐ Writing

Here are some activities to give you an opportunity to practise the skills you have learnt in Chapters 6–9. Remember that there are some things you should always do when you create a piece of writing:

- Plan what you want to write.

- When you are planning, think about why you are writing. What kind of writing is it? What is its purpose?

- Use capital letters and full stops to begin and end sentences.

- Choose the best adjectives and adverbs you can to make your writing interesting.

- Use paragraphs (or verses in a poem) to divide up your ideas.

- Check your work at the end for any silly mistakes.

If you need a reminder about the particular features of the different types of writing, here are some top tips:

- **Explanation texts**: Break up your work into small, clear steps and use vocabulary specific to the topic.

- **Diaries**: Include plenty of feelings and describe what happened in detail. Write in the first person and in the past tense.

- **Scripts**: Remember that you don't need to use speech marks, but don't forget stage directions in brackets.
- **Newspaper reports**: The first paragraph should summarise the whole story. Remember to include interviews with people involved in the story. You could also look at the newspaper report that you read earlier in this chapter.

Now try these tasks to practise the different types of writing.

29 How are animals protected from extinction? Do some research on this topic and write an explanation text. Don't forget to use subheadings.

30 Imagine you have been on a safari holiday or visited a safari park. Write a diary entry about the day. Include how it felt to see so many different animals.

31 Write a short play about visiting a zoo.

32 Write a newspaper article about a wild animal. Perhaps a baby animal is born in a zoo, an animal escapes from a safari park, or a new animal is discovered.

Glossary

This table lists the literary, grammatical and punctuation techniques that you have come across throughout the book and briefly describes what they are.

Adjective	An adjective is a word used to describe a noun.
Adverb	Adverbs often end in -ly and describe verbs. They describe how or when something was done.
Alliteration	Alliteration is the use of a string of words that all start with the same sound.
Apostrophes for contraction	In contractions, an apostrophe is used to show where the missing letter or letters should be. For example, 'they're' is short for 'they are'.
Apostrophes for possession	In order to show that something belongs to someone or something, you need to use apostrophes. For example, 'the boy's laziness' and 'St James' Church'.
Clause	Sentences are made up of clauses. A clause is a part of a sentence with a verb in it. A single-clause sentence has one clause in it. For example: I ate my dinner. A multi-clause sentence has more than one clause in it. For example: I finished my homework and then I played netball.
Comma	A comma is a punctuation mark indicating a pause. Among its many uses are separating items in a list.
Conjunctions	Conjunctions are words (or phrases) that link ideas together and show a relationship between ideas. They include: while, moreover, however and although.
Exclamation marks	Exclamation marks are used at the end of sentences instead of full stops. They are used to show strong emotion, to show when something is being shouted or emphasised and at the end of single-word sentences.
First and third person	If a story is written in the first person, it means that one of the characters in the story is telling the story. If a story is written in the third person, it means it is written from the point of view of a narrator who is not part of the story.
Full stop	A full stop is used to mark the end of a sentence.

Homophones	Homophones are words that sound the same but are spelled differently and have different meanings.
Multi-clause sentence	A multi-clause sentence has more than one part or idea.
Noun	A noun is the name of a person, a place or a thing. Common nouns are the general names of things. 'Hat' and 'coat' are common nouns. Proper nouns are the words for specific, one-of-a-kind places, people or things. They always begin with a capital letter. 'Anne' and 'Great Britain' are proper nouns. A collective noun is a noun for a group of similar things. For example, a group of lions is called a 'pride'.
Past tense	The simple past tense is usually formed by adding -ed to the verb. For example: I walked to the shop. The present perfect tense shows that an event has passed and finished. It uses the verb 'have' before the simple past of the main verb. For example: I have walked to the shop hundreds of times in the past.
Plural	When there is more than one of a noun, we use a plural version of the noun. For example, 'rabbit' becomes 'rabbits'.
Prefix	A prefix is a group of letters added to the beginning of a word.
Preposition	A preposition is a word showing position or direction. In a sentence, prepositions are found before a noun. For example, 'at' is the preposition in 'The dog barked at its owner'.
Question mark	A question mark instead of a full stop is used at the end of a sentence that is a question.
Sentence	A sentence is a group of words that are connected to each other but not to any words outside the sentence.
Speech marks	Speech marks – " " or ' ' – are used to mark the words that are spoken by someone in a piece of writing like a story or a report. They are sometimes called quotation marks or inverted commas.
Suffix	A suffix is a group of letters added to the end of a word.
Synonym	A synonym is a different word with the same meaning.
Verb	A verb is an action or a doing word. For example, 'barked' is the verb in the following sentence: The dog barked at its owner.

Index